Achieving ISO/IEC 20000
Management decisions
and documentation

D1316646

The 'Achieving ISO/IEC 20000' series

This publication is the first in a series of ten publications related to ISO/IEC 20000. Each publication provides advice on different aspects of ISO/IEC 20000. The books in the 'Achieving ISO/IEC 20000' series are:

Management decisions and documentation (BIP 0030)

Why people matter (BIP 0031)

Making metrics work (BIP 0032)

Managing end-to-end service (BIP 0033)

Finance for service managers (BIP 0034)

Enabling change (BIP 0035)

Keeping the service going (BIP 0036)

Capacity management (BIP 0037)

Integrated service management (BIP 0038)

The differences between BS 15000 and ISO/IEC 20000 (BIP 0039)

This series provides practical guidance and advice on introducing IT service management best practice in accordance with ISO/IEC 20000. More details on the content of each publication are given in *Books in the 'Achieving ISO/IEC 20000' series*, at the end of this book.

Although security issues are covered in ISO/IEC 20000, the 'Achieving ISO/IEC 20000' series does not cover security requirements. Information on security can be found in the BSI publications that are listed in the *Bibliography* in Appendix B.

Other publications

BSI also publishes:

A managers' guide to service management (BIP 0005) is intended for managers who are new to support services or who are faced with major changes to their existing support facility. This book takes the form of informative explanations, guidance and recommendations.

IT service management – Self-assessment workbook (BIP 0015) is an easy to use checklist that complements ISO/IEC 20000 and is designed to assist an organization's internal assessment of their services and the extent to which they conform to the specified requirements in ISO/IEC 20000.

Achieving ISO/IEC 20000 Management decisions and documentation

Dr Jenny Dugmore and Shirley Lacy

Business
Information

First published in the UK in 2004

Second edition published in the UK in 2006

by
BSI
389 Chiswick High Road
London W4 4AL

Typeset in Frutiger by Typobatics Limited
Printed in Great Britain by Formara Limited

British Library Cataloguing in Publication Data
A catalogue record for this book is available from the British Library
ISBN 0 580 47458 5

Contents

Foreword

It is acknowledged that service management processes, running in parallel with technology, can make or break the quality of a service and in many cases provide the differentiator between business competitors. Generally, the largest percentage of IT spend in an organization is on the day-to-day support costs, which are in turn strongly influenced by the effectiveness of service management processes.

This climate has created a need for independent methods of assessing the quality and management of services. A leading example is the first international quality standard for service management, ISO/IEC 20000. ISO/IEC 20000 was based on BS 15000, which has been withdrawn.

ISO/IEC 20000 also represents international recognition that service management is an international business with supply chains crossing national boundaries.

Using best practice service management and achieving ISO/IEC 20000 means that senior IT managers 'walk the talk', as their leadership makes or breaks the ability of the whole service provider to achieve best practice.

Dr Jenny Dugmore

Acknowledgements

This book has been produced with the input and assistance of people involved in the practical aspects of delivering services across all sectors. We would like to thank them for sharing their views on the management aspects of ISO/IEC 20000 and for their patience in providing constructive criticism, case studies and suggestions.

It is not possible to list all those who have helped us but particular thanks goes to:

Alison Holt of Synergy International; Barbara Eastman; Bridget Veitch of Xansa; Colin Hamilton of Renard Consulting Ltd; Darcie Destito of Affiliated Computer Services Inc; Don Page of Marval; Lynda Cooper of Fox IT; Majid Iqbal of Carnegie Mellon University; Paul Breslin of DNV Certification; Penny Jeffreys; Peter Lickiss; Sharon Hampton of Serco Solutions; Sharon Taylor of Aspect Group Inc.; Sonia Yusuf; and Steve Abrahams of Siemens Business Services,.

Finally, we would like to thank Simone Levy and Kieran Parkinson of BSI for their support, helpful suggestions and patience during the production of this first book in the 'Achieving ISO/IEC 20000' series.

INTRODUCTION

What is ISO/IEC 20000?

ISO/IEC 20000 is the first IT service management process standard to be produced by the International Organization for Standardization (ISO), and it is based on the knowledge and experience gained by experts working in the field.

ISO/IEC 20000 was produced by Technical Committee ISO/IEC JTC 1/SC 7, *Software and system engineering*, and was based on BS 15000, which was produced by BSI Technical Committee BDD/3, *Information services management*.

ISO/IEC 20000 is in two parts.

- ISO/IEC 20000-1 is a specification containing requirements that must be met in order to achieve ISO/IEC 20000.
- ISO/IEC 20000-2 is a code of practice on how to achieve the requirements in ISO/IEC 20000-1.

The requirements in Part 1 (i.e. ISO/IEC 20000-1) are applicable to service providers of all sizes and types, regardless of whether the organization is public or private sector, internal or external. The recommendations in Part 2 (i.e. ISO/IEC 20000-2) are optional approaches to achieving the requirements in Part 1. Although optional, the recommendations are also practical and proven methods that are normally appropriate.

The purpose of ISO/IEC 20000

ISO/IEC 20000 provides the basis for assessing whether service providers have best practice, reliable, repeatable and measurable processes applied consistently across their organization. As a process-based standard the requirements are independent of organizational structure or of the tools used to automate the service management processes. ISO/IEC 20000-1 provides the basis for formal certification schemes and other audits.

The 'Achieving ISO/IEC 20000' series

The 'Achieving ISO/IEC 20000' series is designed to explain the requirements of ISO/IEC 20000. An abstract of the ISO/IEC 20000 clauses that are most relevant to the topic of management decisions and documentation is given in Appendix A. Also, Table 1 provides a clause-by-clause guide to the content of each of the books in the 'Achieving ISO/IEC 2000' series.

This first publication in the 'Achieving ISO/IEC 20000' series describes the topics of particular relevance to a manager considering the benefits and disadvantages of achieving ISO/IEC 20000. It describes the role of management and the decisions they are faced with if their organizations are to achieve compliance with ISO/IEC 20000.

This publication will assist managers in deciding if the standard is appropriate for their organization by outlining what is involved in making improvements, the roles and responsibilities of management, the types of assessment schemes available, what is required and how to prepare for an audit. It includes a chapter on the use of ISO/IEC 20000 in the procurement process and the terms and definitions that have a specific meaning in ISO/IEC 20000 which must be understood in order for ISO/IEC 20000 to be understood.

It is important for a manager to understand what is required in order to achieve ISO/IEC 20000, including the role of management in the process. This publication includes:

- the benefits of achieving ISO/IEC 20000;
- the relationships between ISO/IEC 20000 and other methods, frameworks of standards;
- the role of management;
- preparation of a business case;
- certification schemes;
- preparation for an audit and audit evidence;
- use of ISO/IEC 20000 in procurement.

Additional advice

Organizations aiming for ISO/IEC 20000 may find it useful to seek advice on best practice, the qualifications that available for individual service management professionals and ISO/IEC 20000 certification. Details of these can be found via the web pages in Appendix B.

Table 1 – Clause-by-clause guide to the 'Achieving ISO/IEC 20000' series

ISO/IEC 20000 clause	BIP 0030	BIP 0031	BIP 0032	BIP 0033	BIP 0034	BIP 0035	BIP 0036	BIP 0037	BIP 0038	BIP 0039
Terms and definitions	▓									▓
Management responsibility	▓								▓	▓
Documentation requirements		▓								▓
Competence, awareness and training									▓	▓
Planning and implementing service management									▓	▓
Plan – Do – Check – Act cycle									▓	
Planning and implementing new or changed services										▓
Service level management				▓						
Service reporting			▓							
Service continuity and availability management							▓			
Budgeting and accounting for IT services					▓					
Information security management	See BSI publications on information security management in the BIP 0070 series									
Capacity management								▓		
Business relationship management				▓						
Supplier management				▓						
Incident management							▓			
Problem management							▓			
Configuration management						▓				
Change management						▓				
Release management						▓				▓

CHAPTER 1

The scope of ISO/IEC 20000

The aim of effective service management is to deliver high levels of customer service and customer satisfaction. Management responsibilities, the Plan-Do-Check-Act (PDCA) cycle and the relationship to service management processes are all essential for achieving ISO/IEC 20000. These concepts are fundamental for setting up sustainable and continually improving service management practices and they establish alignment with the ISO 9000 series of standards.

ISO/IEC 20000 covers the following four aspects:

1) Management responsibilities (clause 3);

2) Planning and implementing service management (clause 4);

3) Planning and implementing new or changed services (clause 5);

4) Service management processes (clauses 6 to 10).

Management responsibilities

The specific requirements on management and management involvement in ISO/IEC 20000 cover:

- management responsibilities;
- documentation requirements, described in Chapter 8;
- competence, awareness and training, described in BIP 0031, *Why people matter*.

The core service management processes are not adequate, in isolation, to achieve the requirements of ISO/IEC 20000.

Management responsibilities

As described in more detail in BIP 0038, *Integrated service management*, the role of management is fundamental to achieving ISO/IEC 20000. This is in part due to the rate of major changes, such as enterprise applications, e-business, mergers and acquisitions, which have in turn meant that some service providers have been in permanent fire-fighting mode. In addition, there is an increase in electronic fraud and the greater dependency on IT and technology enabled services has increased the potential impact of disasters and other events such as terrorist attacks. Regulatory bodies are now mandating stricter control over processes and information.

In this climate, many service providers are not only adopting best practice service management but also providing independent proof of these initiatives. Certification against ISO/IEC 20000 is one method of providing this verification.

Accountability and process ownership

Management responsibilities include demonstrating commitment to best practice service management by accepting that they are accountable for service management overall, and accountable for each of the processes, including the PDCA cycle.

ISO/IEC 20000 requires the appointment of a 'senior responsible owner' who is accountable for the service and service management plan. There is also a requirement that each process is owned by a manager accountable for its quality, with the seniority and sufficient management backing to influence the effective operation of the process. This must extend to ensure the processes are properly integrated (often across organizational boundaries) with a suitable flow of information and with interfaces managed.

Governance

The establishment of successful service management processes within an organization are a critical aspect of governance and an organization's overall governance, particularly with regards to disclosure and financial reporting. Governance integrates and institutionalizes good practices for planning and organizing, acquiring and implementing, delivering and supporting, and monitoring performance. This helps to ensure that the organization's information and related technology supports its business objectives. Governance thus enables the organization to take full advantage of its information, thereby maximizing benefits, capitalizing on opportunities and gaining competitive advantage.

Governance for IT services provides the structure that links IT policies, processes, resources and information to the organization's strategies and objectives. There is now recognition of the benefits of ISO/IEC 20000 in this process. A service provider can demonstrate that the service management requirements of ISO/IEC 20000 have been achieved by certification under a formal ISO/IEC 20000 audit.

Planning and implementing service management

Planning and implementing service management are covered by a requirement for the methodology known as Plan-Do-Check-Act (PDCA), illustrated in Figure 1. This is comparable to the PDCA cycle in the ISO 9000 series. The relationship between ISO/IEC 20000 and ISO 9000 is described in Chapter 3.

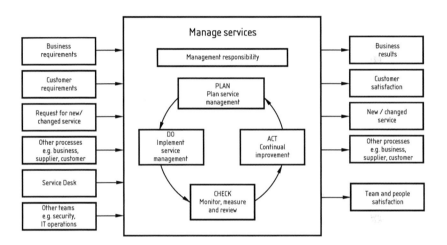

Figure 1 – Plan-Do-Check-Act for service management processes

The PDCA methodology is part of the overall management system. The aim of PDCA is to ensure that the service management processes are properly implemented, integrated and continuously improved.

The PDCA objectives are:

- **Plan:** *To plan the implementation and delivery of service management.*
- **Do:** *To implement the service management objectives and plan.*
- **Check:** *To monitor, measure and review that the service management objectives and plan are being achieved.*
- **Act:** *To improve the effectiveness and efficiency of service delivery and management.*

Adopting the PDCA methodology also prevents the pitfall of implementing service management processes 'bottom-up', where individual processes are at risk of being performed in isolation of each other. For example, implementation of the problem management process without an interface to the change management process, and vice versa, is not best practice however effective the individual processes might be otherwise. The failings of 'bottom-up' implementation are even greater if individual processes are implemented inconsistently across different parts of a service provider's organization.

Those aiming to achieve ISO/IEC 20000, or intending to request it of their service provider, need to recognize the PDCA cycle as an integral part of best practice service management and the ISO/IEC 20000 requirements.

Planning and implementing new or changed services

This aspect covers the requirements in clause 5 of ISO/IEC 20000 and includes requirements for the planning and implementation of new or changed services, with the objective of ensuring that new services and changes to services will be deliverable and manageable at the right cost and service quality. This requires a high standard of planning, including planning for closure of a service. Changes to the established service management processes must also be included in the plan.

The service management processes

This covers the requirements in clause 6 onwards of ISO/IEC 20000 and specifies requirements for the service management processes illustrated in Figure 2. The distinctions between policy, process and procedure as used in ISO/IEC 20000 are given in Chapter 10 and described in more detail in BIP 0039, *Integrated service management*.

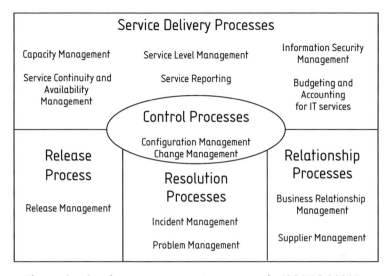

Figure 2 – Service management processes in ISO/IEC 20000

Each of the processes illustrated in Figure 2 could be implemented in isolation as each process offers opportunities for improved service management. However, coordinated implementation of all processes offers greater benefits. Often processes cannot meet the requirements of ISO/IEC 20000 unless the interfaces between processes are understood and the processes are integrated, as the output from one process forms input to another. ISO/IEC 20000 specifically requires interfaces between processes to be understood and managed. Too long a delay in implementing all processes can undermine those implemented already.

Other key aspects

Organizational structure

Service management processes require the service provider to have staff with appropriate skills and clear roles and responsibilities. They need to be well organized and coordinated. However, there are no requirements for specific organizational structure in ISO/IEC 20000 and organizations that meet the requirements of ISO/IEC 20000 may have widely differing structures. This is described in more detail in BIP 0031, *Why people matter.*

Automation

ISO/IEC 20000 does not specify that a service provider must have tools to support processes as the standard focuses on the processes being best practice, and not on the resources, such as tools, used to support the processes. However, most service providers will find that achieving ISO/IEC 20000 is impractical without some tools to make the processes efficient. ISO/IEC20000 may be used by tool providers to assist with the design, so that tools they provider supports best practice service management, although ISO/IEC 20000 does not apply to the actual tools.

Terms and definitions

When using ISO/IEC 20000 it is necessary to understand the terminology. Most words are used with the meaning found in commonly available English language dictionaries. However, some terms in ISO/IEC 20000 have special meanings and are defined in ISO/IEC 20000-1, 2. These are duplicated in Chapter 10.

A number of terms relating to international standards (code of practice, compliance, certification, shall, should, NOTE etc.) are used in this 'Achieving ISO/IEC 20000' series and in ISO/IEC 20000. The reader who is unfamiliar with the precise meaning of these terms will find the explanations in Chapter 10 useful.

BS 15000 and ISO/IEC 20000

Fast-track

ISO/IEC 20000 was based on BS 15000, and was adopted under a fast track process. BS 15000 was put forward for the fast-track process because service management is an international activity and BS 15000, having been produced as a national standard by the UK, had been adopted internationally. Many of those certified against BS 15000 were outside the UK, and many were organizations operating multi-nationally.

During the fast-track process changes were made to the actual requirements, recommendations, terminology, structure and format. This is described in detail in BIP 0039, *The differences between ISO/IEC 20000 and BS 15000*. This publication was based on the change log kept during the drafting of ISO/IEC 20000 and is intended to simply the transition for organizations that had already used BS 15000.

One of the simpler changes was to the name, where *IT service management* became *Information technology – service management*, followed by the Part number and Part name. This was due to differences in naming conventions between national and international standards and has not affected the scope or applicability of the standard.

The name is also included in French: *Technologies de l'information — Gestion de services — Partie 2: Code de bonne pratique*

What does ISO/IEC signify?

In discussions, standards are often referred to informally using only their individual numbers or the numbers associated with a series of standards. For example, '15000', '20000', '9000', '14000' and '27000'.

The coding of ISO/IEC is significant and should be used for all but informal purposes.

ISO (the International Organization for Standardization) and IEC (the International Electrotechnical Commission) are the international bodies responsible for worldwide standardization.

ISO and IEC technical committees collaborate in fields of mutual interest and national standards bodies that are members of ISO or IEC will participate in the development of standards. In the field of information technology, ISO and IEC have established a joint technical committee ISO/IEC JTC 1 and within this committee SC 7 is responsible for the management and enhancement of ISO/IEC 20000.

It is the role of the joint committee (ISO and IEC) that is signified by the name of the standard; it is incorrect to refer to ISO/IEC 20000 as ISO 20000. Being a JTC 1/SC 7 standard influences how the standard will be developed.

Some international standards, such as ISO 9000, are solely the responsibility of ISO, so the use of only ISO in ISO 9000 is correct.

What about the date?

The first edition of both parts of ISO/IEC 20000 were published on 15th December 2005. On this date BS 15000 was superseded and withdrawn from the lists of valid UK standards.

The convention for international standards is that if the date is not shown, the most recent version is implied. In the case of this first edition the year implied is 2005. The bibliography for both parts[1] of ISO/IEC 20000 show 16 standards listed without reference to the year of publication, in each case the most recent edition is implied.

There are circumstances where it is essential for the year to be shown – for example, on web pages listing available standards – and certificates awarded following a formal certification audit should always reference the year of publication for the avoidance of doubt over what the audit covered.

---

[1] The role of each part is described in the Introduction to each publication in the 'Achieving ISO/IEC 20000' series.

For example, the two parts of ISO/IEC 20000 would be shown on an audit certificate as:

- ISO/IEC 20000:2005 — Information technology — Service management — Part 1: Specification.

What is a national implementation?

Each national standards body may publish what is referred to as a national implementation. This was done by BSI on the same date as ISO/IEC 20000 was published – 15th December 2005. The correct name for national implementation by the UK is:

- BS ISO/IEC 20000:2005 — Information technology — Service management — Part 1: Specification; and

- BS ISO/IEC 20000:2005 — Information technology — Service management — Part 2: Code of practice.

National implementations include a national foreword and national annex/bibliography. In the case of the UK national implementation the annex and foreword have been used to include references to BSI publications and ITIL, since formatting rules for international standards allow only ISO and ISO/IEC standards to be listed in a standard such as ISO/IEC 20000. Permission to use copyright material from any part or clause of ISO/IEC 20000 may be obtained via the national standards body as well as by application to ISO.

In ISO/IEC 20000-1 (and similarly in national implementations) only clauses 3 to 10 are relevant to compliance, as it is only these clauses that contain the word 'shall', used to signify the requirements that must be met (details of terms in standards are given in Chapter 10).

Irrespective of whether the service provider or audit company purchased their copy of ISO/IEC 20000 from BSI (as BS ISO/IEC 20000) or the core ISO/IEC version from ISO, audits are against the requirements in Part 1 clauses 3 to 10 and the certificate will show ISO/IEC 20000:2005 — Information technology — Service management — Part 1: Specification.

CHAPTER 2

Why ISO/IEC 20000?

There are many reasons for an organization not only to implement the requirements specified in ISO/IEC 20000, but also to aim for a full certification audit. The key benefits are described below.

Creating organizational goals

Few service providers, either internal or external, operate in a stable environment with highly satisfied customers, highly skilled and motivated staff and increased budgets. On the contrary, many service providers are dependent on complex supply chains, face frequent changes, reduced budgets and demands for better services. Many service providers will also face customer complaints about service levels. Problems arise due to high staff turnover or staff who are de-motivated.

Very few service providers face all these challenges at the same time, but a service provider that adopts ISO/IEC 20000 as a quality goal will be better equipped to deal with them if they arise.

- ISO/IEC 20000 can be used to create organizational goals for service improvements and, if implemented correctly, the service providers will be able to provide documented proof of delivered improvements.

- ISO/IEC 20000 establishes a basis for comparison with other service providers by generating benchmarking information.

- Service providers that are already certified to other management system standards, such as ISO 9000, can also aim for ISO/IEC 20000. Implementation of ISO/IEC 20000 requirements can provide specific improvements over a broad base of activities.

- Proctor & Gamble has saved about $500 million across multiple departments from streamlining processes with ITIL®[2]. Although there are no figures in the public domain yet for those for those achieving ISO/IEC 20000, service providers can expect to make significant savings.

Baselining and benchmarking

Many service providers are required to, or choose to be, baselined and/or benchmarked. Baselining allows the service provider to monitor the changes in quality of its processes and services over a period of time. It is an internal comparison of key aspects of the service, workloads and service management processes, often measured before and after a change (e.g. a programme of service improvements). Benchmarking allows the comparison to be made to industry norms based on the performance of other similar service providers or independent standard such as ISO/IEC 20000.

Baselining and benchmarking are described in more detail in BIP 0032, *Making metrics work*.

There are various reasons why a service provider may opt for baselining or benchmarking, these include:

- meeting government requirements for public sector organizations;
- meeting regulatory requirements, e.g. food and drink, financial and pharmaceutical industries;
- proving they are suitable as a supplier and to ensure that they are competitive.

For commercial suppliers, certification to standards such as ISO/IEC 20000 provides a significant competitive advantage and may be required as part of their contract with a customer. In today's world, standards certification is becoming less of an option and more of a necessity.

Common processes

As described in BIP 0033, *Managing end-to-end services*, many service providers operate as a link in a complex supply chain with multiple suppliers and multiple customer groups. Service providers will have distributed service management processes where a variation in process could cause confusion and unnecessary management overheads.

---

[2] ITIL (IT Infrastructure Library) is a registered trade mark of OGC (the Office of Government Commerce).

If each organization in a supply chain operates with the same high standard of service management, using a common terminology, the inter-organizational processes will be more effective and the deliverables at each stage of the chain will be more reliable. The same benefits can be obtained by a single service provider having consistent service management processes throughout its organization.

One notable benefit from the standardization of service management processes is reduced risk and cost of using external organizations as suppliers.

It becomes easier to select service providers using ISO/IEC 20000 as part of the procurement process (as described in Chapter 8) and easier to manage across a diverse technical environment when processes are consistent and independent of the type of technology.

Benefits to the customer

One of the biggest benefits is to the customer in the form of a speedier and enhanced quality of service. There will also be controlled and reduced long-term costs of service delivery arising from the rigour and efficiency of best practice processes. More consistency in the processes makes them more predictable leading to improved customer satisfaction.

If an internal service provider has met the requirements specified in ISO/IEC 20000, their internal customers are more likely to have a competitive edge over their competitors as they in turn will be able to deliver an improved service and adapt more effectively to meet new business needs.

Example: Local government council

A local government council was aware that it had a number of IT issues, including network problems that took too long to resolve, a desktop roll out that had created many problems and a helpdesk that could not resolve user incidents at the time of the call. They also recognized that their ability to manage problems and incidents was inefficient. Overall, they were not delivering the level of service that users needed or expected.

During migration from a mainframe environment to client-server environment, they anticipated an increase in the number of changes leading to higher call volumes (and therefore higher risk to the service). They recognized the need for rapid improvements to, and tighter control over, their service management processes. Management also recognized the need for change to the organizational structure and the need to raise the morale of badly de-motivated staff.

Management decided to use ISO/IEC 20000 as a service improvement goal in order to facilitate these changes. By utilizing best practice processes ISO/IEC 20000 enabled the council to:

- implement e-government more effectively;

- support electronic service delivery more effectively;

- improve efficiency and effectiveness in preparation for value for money reviews;

- prepare to plan and implement government driven initiatives such as euro compatibility.

They have also observed that aiming for ISO/IEC 20000 certification has helped transform their reactive helpdesk to a proactive service desk that can:

- deliver confidence in their IT service levels among their end users;

- improve customer satisfaction and provide a more reliable service;

- resolve most incidents at the time of the first call, providing a fast and cost-effective solution;

- be properly supported by other processes and support teams, improving the overall efficiency.

Key point:

They were able to make major improvements using ISO/IEC 20000, with the benefits outweighing the costs of improvements and other changes. The staff are now better motivated and more confident of their ability to meet the customer's needs.

Example: Service management consultancy

A service management consultancy started to use ISO/IEC 20000 as a quality and service improvement goal for their own internal IT services even before a certification scheme was established. Even without a certification scheme they found the use of ISO/IEC 20000 beneficial.

The key message was that it has made them move from an 'ought to' to a 'can do' organizational philosophy. ISO/IEC 20000 also enabled them to establish more reliable processes, in particular reducing the risk of failed changes and the subsequent costs of the incident management process.

Customer satisfaction was reported to have improved as a consequence of the improvements to the service. They also recognized that adopting best practices was not an optional or unrealistic ideal but had to be the norm for everyone involved in the provision of service management. The management realized that they had to demonstrate commitment by being more proactive and involved with best practice processes and not simply leaving this to their staff in isolation.

Key point:

This organization recommends ISO/IEC 20000 as a quality and service improvement goal and are now planning to undergo a certification audit.

Example: Financial organization

An organization in the finance sector operates in an area where there is a high service focus. Their internal service provider aims for service excellence, which they see as one of the ways they can differentiate themselves. They recognised that achieving compliance with ISO/IEC 20000 would provide them with a real focus to consistently achieve an appropriate standard of service management. Once they had reached this level they would not want to fall back into 'bad habits', so it would give them a real incentive to continuously improve.

Use of ISO/IEC 20000 gave them a focus and the confidence that they were applying some parts of service management the right way. Self-assessment against ISO/IEC 20000, using BIP 0015, *IT service management – Self-assessment workbook*, provided them with a benchmark to plan improvements. They found that in practice two people could cover all processes in one week. They interviewed staff and completed the questions during the interview. They found it was difficult to be impartial, as the internal auditors would want to register a positive result even if the process/aspect in question was short of the mark. As a result they would recommend that organizations use an independent assessor. They believe it would also be better if the assessor was an external expert on service management as this would help gain more credibility for the results.

Key point:

By starting with internal self-assessment the organization was able to plan service improvements effectively.

CHAPTER 3

Other standards and best practices

There are wide range of standards, best practices and methodologies that could be seen as being complementary or alternatives to ISO/IEC 20000.

They all provide distinct advantages and many will work well if used in addition to ISO/IEC 20000.

It is important to understand what each alternative provides and how it may be combined with ISO/IEC 20000 to give additional benefits to existing processes and systems. It is not possible to cover every one of these in this publication, however, some of the major standards and methodologies are compared in this section. These are ITIL, ISO 9000, ISO/IEC 17799 and the '27000 series', eSCM-SP Deming Cycle and CobIT.

IT Infrastructure Library (ITIL)

ITIL is a service management framework developed by the UK Office of Government Commerce (OGC). ITIL provides best practice guidelines, advice and options that can be selectively adopted and adapted to suit local circumstances and business needs. Although developed in the UK it is used world-wide by private and public sector organizations.

ITIL dates back to the late 1980s, initially concentrating on infrastructure management. Successive titles were published through the 1990s as the focus moved to IT Service Management. Between 2000 and 2004 the earlier material was updated and rationalized into seven core books, although supporting titles continue to appear.

At the time of publication of this publication ITIL is undergoing a 'refresh programme' the aim of which is to improve the content of the publications and the usefulness and applicability of ITIL. This will deliver improvements required in structure, business focus etc.

In the mid-1990s a concordat was signed between British Standards Institution (BSI), itSMF and the OGC. This formed the basis for cooperation and positioning of publications so that they are part of the same logical structure. The logical relationship still applies to ITIL and ISO/IEC 20000, as shown in Figure 3. The current relationship between ITIL and ISO/IEC 20000 is shown in Figure 3.

ITIL will reflect a life stage approach, with the first step service strategy. This is compatible with the importance of management commitment and policies representing management direction in ISO/IEC 20000.

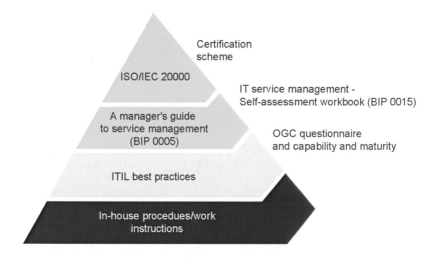

Figure 3 – ITIL and ISO/IEC 20000

It is envisaged that ITIL and ISO/IEC 20000 will continue to develop in step with each other and will continue to be adopted by organizations hoping to achieve a wide range of different goals.

Although they are aligned, ITIL and the ISO/IEC 20000 series serve different purposes.

The prime purpose of ISO/IEC 2000-1 is to provide best practice standard that is suitable for independent third-party certification audits. By its nature ITIL does not provide the basis for an independent third-party certification audit.

It is not a requirement for a service provider to have adopted ITIL best practices or ITIL terminology to achieve ISO/IEC 20000. However, it will certainly be easier to achieve if this is the case. Even though there is a close link between ISO/IEC 20000 and ITIL, there are a few differences, as follows.

Table 2 – Comparison of ISO/IEC 20000 and ITIL

ISO/IEC 20000	ITIL
Organizational structure	
The requirements are completely independent of organizational structure. A service provider must use the structure that is most appropriate for efficient service.	ITIL includes advice and cites alternative options for some aspects of organizational structure.
Organizational size	
The standard applies to all sizes of organization. How each size and type of organization meets the requirements may be different. An auditor will use professional judgment to decide if the approach adopted by the service provider is appropriate for the size of organization. The standard requires a 'fit for purpose' approach, for example a small service provider may need a relatively simple capacity plan and policies, a large one may need a more complex and sophisticated approach.	Most of the advice can be adapted to meet the needs of different sized organizations. The differing circumstances of organizations of different types and sizes is also a feature of the current ITIL refresh programme. Specialist advice is available for small organizations. ITIL includes advice on the activities of a Service Desk that can be adapted for all sizes of organizations.
Organizational sector	
The standard applies to both commercial and in-house service providers and the requirements are scoped to reflect this applicability. For example, the agreement between supplier and customer is not required to be contractual as some service providers are part of the same organization as their customer. As they are part of the same legal entity there cannot be a legally binding contract between them. In contrast, a service provider's arrangement with an external supplier must be contractual if the supplier is a separate legal entity. This is described in more detail in BIP 0033, *Managing end-to-end services*.	ITIL origins were best practice advice for the UK Government, but has over the years evolved to be best practice for all sectors, including organizations that provide services to UK Government, and organizations that are private sector or outside the UK. As a consequence ITIL includes advice on topics that is outside the scope of ISO/IEC 20000, such as charging for services as part of ITIL best practice on financial management.

Table 2 – Comparison of ISO/IEC 20000 and ITIL (*continued*)

ISO/IEC 20000	ITIL
Management system requirements and Plan-Do-Check-Act	
Management responsibilities, the Plan-Do-Check-Act cycle and the relationship to service management processes, are all essential for achieving ISO/IEC 20000. These concepts are fundamental for setting up sustainable and continually improving service management practices under the requirements of ISO/IEC 20000. They also establish alignment with standards such as the '9000 series' and the '27000 series'.	The core of the ITIL best practice advice is targeted at individual processes, to assist organizations understand what they should include in the journey to best practice service management. ITIL includes PDCA cycle (with references to the Deming cycle). By its nature each organization may opt to include or exclude PDCA or individual service management processes, whereas there is no option for achieving ISO/IEC 20000.
Service management processes	
Process groups	
The standard groups processes into five main categories, as shown in Figure 2. These are service delivery, relationship, resolution, control and release management processes. The grouping of processes is not part of the requirements and was done largely on the basis of common interfaces. A service provider may group processes differently (or not group them at all). The difference in grouping between the standard and ITIL is not of importance for certification or for adoption of ITIL best practices.	Most processes are currently grouped by publication, as either service support or service delivery, with some processes (such as information security management) as separate publications. Service continuity and availability management are currently separate processes in ITIL. At the time this publication is to be printed there is discussion that ITIL refresh may group processes differently, for example, security may be absorbed within ITIL process elements. The ITIL refresh is expected to group processes under a life stages model.
Relationship management processes	
Includes business relationship management and supplier management processes, which are not covered by the main ITIL (Service Support and Service Delivery) books.	Aspects of additional processes for business relationship management and supplier management are covered by current and planned OGC publications.
Service reporting	
Service reporting is a separate service management process. It is key to service management, the PDCA cycle and the integration of processes.	Some processes make reference to service reports, particularly service level management. However, service reporting is not treated as a separate process.

Table 2 – Comparison of ISO/IEC 20000 and ITIL (*continued*)

ISO/IEC 20000	ITIL
Service continuity and availability management	
Service continuity and availability management are combined into one process. The requirements specified for these processes are closely related and treating them separately results in duplication.	Service continuity and availability management are treated as separate processes.
Budgeting and accounting	
The Part 1 specification includes requirements for budgeting and accounting. Charging is not applicable for some organizations so cannot be included in the specification.	Advice on best practice financial management, including charging, is included.
Information security management	
Includes requirements for information security management processes. A note in Part 1 refers to ISO/IEC 17799, a code of practice for security requirements. (Notes do not change the requirements nor do they affect the scope of an audit.)	ITIL includes a Security Management Guide, although there is limited alignment between this publication and ISO/IEC 17799 or ISO/IEC 27001 (both are described in the section comparing ISO/IEC 20000 to Security standards). ITIL refresh is expected to refer to formal standards, such as the ISO/IEC 27000 series.
Capacity management	
Capacity management covers the planning for and management of all types of capacity, i.e. software, hardware, storage, infrastructure, people, facilities. The standard draws no distinction between different types but does require the service provider to be able to view capacity and performance from the perspective of the whole organization, costs, changes and individual services.	ITIL draws a distinction between resource capacity, service capacity and business capacity management processes.
Configuration and asset management	
Asset management is covered by configuration management, aligning with the ITIL Service Support and Service Delivery books version 2.	ITIL includes advice on software asset management as a separate publication.

ISO 9000

ISO 9000 is a well-established quality management system standard. It is designed to be applicable to all organizations and is therefore much more generic than ISO/IEC 20000.

The term ISO 9000 or even simply '9000' is commonly used to informally describe a series of standards that are closely related.

- ISO 9000 covers the fundamentals and vocabulary of quality (process) management.

- ISO 9001 covers the requirements for quality management systems.

- What was ISO 9003 is now ISO/IEC 90003, covering guidelines for the application of ISO 9001:2000 to computer software.

ISO/IEC 90003 is managed by the same sub-committee as ISO/IEC 20000, i.e ISO/IEC JTC 1/SC7.

ISO 9000 and ISO/IEC 20000 can be compared as follows.

- Both are management systems standards with some overlap in the PDCA cycle.

- ISO 9000 is generic and has a broader scope as it addresses all working practices in an organization.

- ISO/IEC 20000 is tightly focused on service management and is specifically designed to ensure the use of best practice processes for service management. Therefore, ISO/IEC 20000 is most relevant to organizations that wish to target service management processes (this typically represents 80% of IT spend).

If IT service management is fundamental to an organization then it will be more appropriate for it to aim for certification against ISO/IEC 20000 as it is more specific in its requirements than ISO 9000.

ISO/IEC 20000 is not otherwise linked to ISO 9000 and requires a separate certification audit, even if both ISO 9000 and ISO/IEC 20000 audits are carried out at the same time and by the same auditors.

Defining and agreeing the ISO/IEC 20000 audit scope, described in Chapter 5, is an important aspect of achieving ISO/IEC 20000 and the same service provider is likely to find it different to defining an audit scope for ISO 9000. ISO/IEC 20000 includes mandatory requirements for each process and the PDCA cycle. The scope of a ISO/IEC 20000 certification audit cannot be based on an assessment of the processes that are in place. All of those processes included in ISO/IEC 20000 must be in the service provider's scope to some extent. This is in contrast to

ISO 9000, which does not dictate which processes are mandatory but requires whatever processes are present to be of the required standard.

ISO/IEC 17799 and the '27000' series

The 'Achieving ISO/IEC 20000' series does not cover security processes as there are a number of specialist publications that do cover security requirements, including those listed in Appendix B, Bibliography.

Names and numbers

In an earlier and similar fast track process to that followed by BS 15000 to become ISO/IEC 20000, BS 7799, a two part standard on information security management was submitted for fast tracking to become an international standard.

The code of practice was accepted during the voting process and was originally published as ISO/IEC 17799:2000, with a second edition published in 2005 as ISO/IEC 17799:2005, *Information technology — Security techniques — Information security management system — Code of practice*.

The other part of BS 7799, the specification, was considered to require additional development and drafting. The BS 7799 specification continued to be a valid UK standard and was used as the basis of a certification scheme while additional work was done on drafting it to become an international standard.

In late 2005 the first edition of the international specification standard was agreed and published as the first in what is commonly referred to as the '27000 series', ISO/IEC 27001, *Information technology — Security techniques — Information security management system — Requirements*.

Unlike ISO/IEC 20000, the '27000 series' does not use the convention of Part 1 being denoted by '-1' and Part 2 by '-2'. The second part of the '27000 series' will be ISO/IEC 17799 renumbered as ISO/IEC 27002. The renumbering of ISO/IEC 17799 will not happen until April 2007.

The '27000 series' is planned to be five parts, including:

- ISO/IEC 27003, on implementation guidance;

- ISO/IEC 27004, on metrics and measurement;

- ISO/IEC 27005, on risk assessment.

ISO/IEC 20000 links to ISO/IEC 17799

The relationship between ISO/IEC 20000 and security standards is important because the two sets of standards support each other, each bringing benefits. Many of the requirements are compatible, with the security standard including more detailed requirements for information security than ISI/IEC 20000-1.

The most important reference to security standards in the second edition of BS 15000 was a NOTE in BS 15000-1. This NOTE was sometimes misinterpreted as a 'free pass' for those certified against BS 7799, i.e. it was sometimes incorrectly assumed that if a service provider was certified against BS 7799 there would be no need for an audit to be done against the information security management requirements of ISO/IEC 20000, 6.6. This was not correct as a NOTE cannot add to or remove any of the requirements and does itself not form part of the requirements.

The reference to ISO/IEC 17799 in ISO/IEC 20000 is also a NOTE that does not affect the requirements of ISO/IEC 20000-1 or change the scope of what must be audited.

ISO/IEC 17799 is a code of practice, not a suitable basis for an independent certification audit, although an organization may claim compliance with it. Details of the differences between specifications, codes of practice, certification and compliance are explained in Chapter 4. The terms are also included in Chapter 10.

The basis of independent certification audits is ISO/IEC 27001:2005, which contains requirements, but which was published to late in 2005 to be included during the drafting and editing of ISO/IEC 20000.

Security requirements in ISO/IEC 27001

Like ISO/IEC 20000, the requirements specified by ISO/IEC 27001 promote the adoption of a process approach for establishing, implementing, operating, monitoring, maintaining and improving effectiveness. It refers to the PDCA cycle adapted to information security requirements and other management responsibilities are described in some detail. Terms and definitions are inevitably focused on security rather than on service management. Most terms and definitions are specialist security terms, but there are some differences and overlaps with the terms and definitions of ISO/IEC 20000-1, as shown in Table 3.

Table 3 – Terms and usage

ISO/IEC 20000	ISO/IEC 27001
Availability: ability of a component or service to perform its required function at a stated instant or over a stated period of time. NOTE Availability is usually expressed as a ratio of the time that the service is actually available for use by the business to the agreed service hours.	**Availability**: the property of being accessible and usable upon demand by an authorized entity [ISO/IEC 13335-1:2004]
Incident: any event which is not part of the standard operation of a service and which causes or may cause an interruption to, or a reduction in, the quality of that service. NOTE This may include request questions such as "How do I...?" calls. ...*and the closely linked.....* Problem: unknown underlying cause of one or more incidents.	**Information security incident**: a single or a series of unwanted or unexpected information security events that have a significant probability of compromising business operations and threatening information security [ISO/IEC TR 18044:2004]
Information security: is used (but not defined) to mean the process with the objective: *To manage information security effectively within all service activities.*	**Information security**: preservation of confidentiality, integrity and availability of information; in addition, other properties such as authenticity, accountability, non-repudiation and reliability can also be involved [ISO/IEC 17799:2005]

Requirements include compulsory controls and control objectives that cover all aspects of information security. The requirements map onto not only the requirements in ISO/IEC 20000, 6.6, but also to other clauses, as shown in Table 4.

Table 4 – Example requirement mapping

ISO/IEC 20000-1 clause	ISO/IEC 27001 topic mapping
3.2 Documents and records	Disposal of documents and records/media
3.4 Training competence and awareness	Especially of policies
6.1 Service reporting	Metrics and measurements
6.5 Capacity management	Minimizing risk of system failure
7.3 Supplier management	External access controls
8.1 and 8.2 Incident management	Logging/tracking (security) incidents
8.1 and 8.3 Problem management	Learning from incidents
9.2 Change management	Controls to maintain network security
10.1 Release management	Acceptance criteria for systems

Which standard and when?

The scope and detail of ISO/IEC 27001 means it is particularly relevant to any organization that must have proof of security controls for regulatory or legal requirements. For such an organization the best route may be via achieving ISO/IEC 20000, as this provides a broad base of process controls that are compatible with those from ISO/IEC 27001 and which will act as the basis for the greater depth of security controls required by ISO/IEC 27001.

An alternative route could be an intensive programme of activity to meet the requirements of ISO/IEC 27001, followed by broadening of disciplines and good practices to meet the wider scope of ISO/IEC 20000-1.

For organizations where the service provider's core activity is service management for delivery of technology enabled services, achieving ISO/IEC 20000 first (with or without a later programme to meet the requirements of ISO/IEC 27001) is likely to provide the most cost effective route.

The management on the relative merits of achieving either standard, or both and if both, the order they are achieved should be based on:

- an understanding of the business needs of the customer(s);
- the service provider's own needs, if they differ form those of the customer(s);
- the current quality of processes;
- the relative costs of achieving one or both;
- the risks of the programme of changes required;
- the risks of not making the required changes for either or both.

e-Sourcing Capability Model for Service Providers (eSCM-SP)[3]

eSCM-SP includes best practices on both outsourcing and insourcing, and pre-contract and post-contract authorization processes. It is intended to give a multi-level path for capability improvement, innovation and sustenance for sourcing of technology-enabled services. eSCM-SP is targeted at sourcing services that use IT as an enabler for developing service designs, coordinating service deployment and delivering services. It is primarily aimed at commercial service providers where the service will be defined in a legally binding contract. eSCM-SP covers the full life-cycle of outsourcing issues and arrangements, particularly with respect to the management of contracts and personnel. The structure of eSCM-SP is illustrated in Figure 4.

eSCM has the same origins as other capability/maturity models, such as CMM Integration[SM] (CMMI®), and is similar in approach. ISO/IEC 20000 and eSCM-SP are complementary to each other. While ISO/IEC 20000 is a specification which measures compliance with best practice service management, eSCM is used to measure the capability/maturity of a supply chain and to track how this changes over time.

---

[3] Extracts from The eSourcing Capability Model for Service Providers (eSCM-SP) v2 are reproduced with the permission of Carnegie Mellon University, 5000 Forbes Avenue, Pittsburgh, PA 15213, USA.

[SM] CMM Integration is a service mark of Carnegie Mellon University.

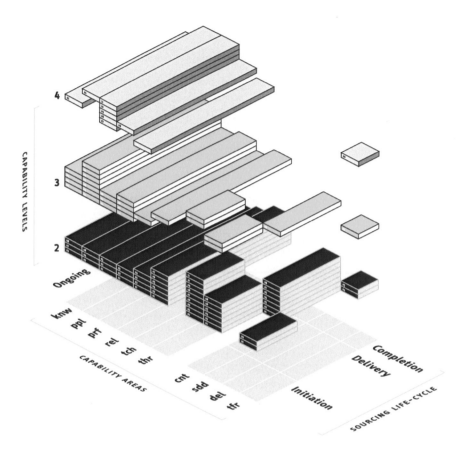

Figure 4 – eSCM structure[4]

Deming Cycle

The Deming Cycle shown below in Figure 5 is usually considered to be the origin of Plan-Do-Check-Act methodology embedded in management system standards like ISO 9000 and ISO/IEC 20000. The Deming Cycle requires:

- well-defined processes and activities to be measured for compliance with expected values;

- outputs to be audited to validate and improve the process.

---

[4] Hyder, Elaine B., Keith Heston, Mark Paulk. April 2004. The Sourcing Capability Model for Service Providers (eSCM-SP) v2, Part 1: Model Overview. CMU-ISRI-04-113. Carnegie Mellon University.

The Deming Cycle requirements are very broad and an organization can create and develop their own approach to improvement. The PDCA aspects of the Deming Cycle can therefore supplement the implementation of any processes required by ISO/IEC 20000.

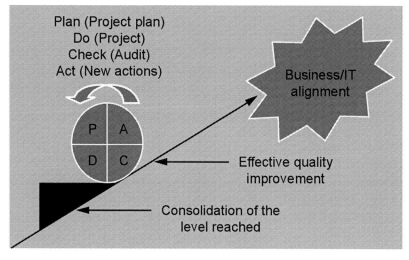

Figure 5 – Deming and PDCA

CObiT® - Control Objectives for Information and related Technology

CObiT was initially created by the Information Systems Audit and Control Foundation in 1996, and the IT Governance Institute updated it in 2000 for the release of the 3rd Edition. Release 4 was published in 2005.

CObiT provides a control and management framework with a set of good practices. It provides the links between IT governance requirements, IT processes and IT controls. It is strongly focused on control and less on execution.

CObiT addresses a broad spectrum of duties in IT management, including significant parts of IT service management. It is based on established frameworks and best practices including the Software Engineering Institute's Capability Maturity Model, ISO 9000, ITIL® and ISO/IEC 17799. There is overlap with standards such as ISO/IEC 20000, ISO/IEC 17799, which is to become part of the ISO/IEC 27000 series and TickIT (TickIT provides a scheme for the certification of software quality management systems).

For IT to be successful in delivering against business requirements, COBIT recommends that management put an internal control system or framework in place that enables IT to be successful in delivering against business requirements. It is relatively high level and broad-based, aiming to be generically complete, but not specific. As a result it is much longer than most specification standards such as ISO/IEC 20000 and ISO/IEC 27001. Technical details are not included and it is based on the assumption that the necessary tasks for complying with the control objectives are self-explanatory.

What organizations are involved?

IT Governance Institute (ITGI)

This was established in 1998 to advance international thinking and standards in directing and controlling an enterprise's information technology. This was done on the basis that effective IT governance helps ensure that IT supports business goals, optimizes business investment in IT, and appropriately manages IT-related risks and opportunities.

The Information Systems Audit and Control Association (ISACA)

Founded in 1969 as the EDP Auditors Association, ISACA is an international professional, technical and educational organization dedicated to being a recognized global leader in IT governance, security, control and assurance. Its membership is targeted at and includes internal and external auditors, CEOs, CFOs, CIOs, educators, information security and control professionals, students and IT consultants.

ISACA offers 'Certified Information Systems Auditor TM (CISA®) designation', for experienced IS audit, control and security professionals. Similarly it offers the 'Certified Information Security Manager®(CISM®)' designation, for leaders who manage information security.

What does COBIT provide?

COBIT provides a number of useful features, many related to the audit practices and ensuring internal controls are working correctly. This includes:

- a common approach for IT functions, the business and auditors;
- strong support for IT audit, reducing the cost of audit risk assessment;

- assistance when implementing effective practices by avoiding the need to 're-invent the wheel'.

ISACA also claim CoBiT is compliant with ISO17799, COSO I and COSO II.

Mapping has been done to many other standards. Recent examples of mapping include to ISO/IEC 17799 and ITIL and to ISO/IEC 20000.

CoBiT Quickstart™

This is intended to assist in rapid and easy adoption of the most essential elements of CoBiT, particularly small and medium sized organizations. ISACA also consider it useful for accelerated adoption of governance best practices for organizations of all sizes.

CoBiT Online™

This is a web-based resource for best practices including downloadable customized guidance and for benchmarking. A variety of subscription levels are available, each allowing different amounts and types of access and functionality.

CoBiT Security Baseline™

This provides the essential steps for implementing information security within the enterprise.

CoBiT Components

CoBiT provides 34 generic processes that manage the IT resources to deliver information to the business according to the business and governance requirements. Primarily of interest to governance, assurance, control and security professionals, the following are main elements of CoBiT.

- **Executive Summary:** explains key concepts and principles.

- **Framework:** the basis of the approach and the foundation for all the other elements. The process model is organized into four domains: Plan and Organize (PO), Acquire and Implement (AI), Deliver and Support (DS), and Monitor and Evaluate (ME).

- **Control objectives:** component provides more than 300 generic control statements that define what needs to be managed in each IT process to address the business requirements of ensuring IT delivers value, risks are managed and requirements are met.

- **Control practices:** provides guidance on why controls are needed and what the best practices are for meeting specific control objectives. Control practices helps ensure that solutions put forward are likely to be more completely and successfully implemented.

- **Management guidelines:** helps IT managers improve IT performance and link IT objectives to business objectives.

- **Audit guidelines:** outlines and suggests which assessment activities should be performed for each of 34 high-level IT control objectives, providing guidance on who to interview, what questions to ask, and how to evaluate control, assess compliance and finally, substantiate the risk of the controls not being met.

- **IT Governance implementation guide:** Provide a generic road map for implementing IT governance using the COBIT resources

Comparison with ISO/IEC 20000

In the context of IT governance COBIT has a focus on the Plan-Do-Check-Act (PDCA) cycle. ISO/IEC 20000 includes the PDCA cycle but also gives emphasis to each service management process, the integration of processes and the relationship between PDCA cycle and service management processes.

COBIT is based on a top-down approach based on a hierarchy of domains, process and activities. This has parallels with the ISO/IEC 20000 top-down policy, process, procedure hierarch.

In COBIT each process is described by using the following information:

- high-level control objectives;

- detailed control objectives;

- information criteria affected by the process;

- IT resources used by the process;

- typical characteristics depending on the maturity level;

- inputs and outputs of the process;

- RACI chart of activities against function (RACI charts are described in BIP 0031, *Why people matter*);

- goals and metrics.

In ISO/IEC 20000 some of the details, such as metrics are left to the judgment of the service provider.

CoBiT processes in the delivery and support domain are covered in a comprehensive manner by ISO/IEC 20000 clauses 6 to 10, there is also some overlap between CoBiT processes, tasks and duties of the domains PO, AI and ME in ISO/IEC 20000 clauses 3 to 5 and clauses 7.3 and 9.2, which cover:

- 3.1 management responsibilities;

- 3.2 documents and records;

- 3.3 competence, awareness and training;

- 4. PDCA cycle;

- 5. Planning and implementing new or changed services;

- 7.3 Supplier management process;

- 9.2 Manage changes.

The audit guidance and practices of CoBiT can provide useful input to an organization planning extensive changes and improvements in order to achieve ISO/IEC 20000 and other related management systems standards such as ISO/IEC 27001 and ISO/IEC 90003.

CHAPTER 4

Compliance and certification audits

There are three methods available for a service provider to verify if they are compliant with the requirements specified in ISO/IEC 20000. These are internal reviews, external reviews/pre-audit reviews and certification audits.

Internal reviews

Staff within the service provider's own organization can carry out an assessment and see if the processes conform to the requirements specified in ISO/IEC 20000. This is usually undertaken as an initial review to provide an assessment of the scale of work required to meet the requirements of ISO/IEC 20000. The reviews may be carried out with variable degrees of rigour, according to the needs of the organization, the maturity of the service management processes and the reasons for the review.

External reviews/pre-audit reviews

This is a similar assessment often carried out by auditors outside of the service provider's organization. These reviews are generally given greater weight due to the independence of the audit. These audits may be similar to the approach and rigour of the certification audits, but they do not lead to formal certification. They may also be carried out as part of a service improvement programme by an organization that does not intend to go through a full certification audit but still wishes to use ISO/IEC 20000-1 as a quality benchmark and using ISO/IEC 20000-2 as a source of advice.

Certification audits

This is an external audit leading to a certificate being awarded, if the service provider is found to have met all the requirements. Certification audits are carried out by professionally qualified auditors.

In the UK, these auditors are accredited under EN 45012 by their relevant national accreditation body, which in turn must be recognized by either the European Cooperation for Accreditation (EA) or The International Accreditation Forum, Inc. (IAF). Similar arrangements exist for other countries. EA or IAF will be able to provide details. More information on EA and IAF is available via their web pages, and both EA and IAF are included in the terms and definitions in Chapter 10.

A qualified auditor will also be able to demonstrate competence in the requirements of ISO/IEC 20000 that are specific to service management processes and requirements. A service provider may seek reassurance about the qualifications of their prospective auditors by asking to see their certificates.

In the context of the needs of the customer, business and regulatory bodies, the auditor is responsible for assessing the:

- suitability of the scope of the audit;
- management responsibilities and controls;
- implementation of the PDCA cycle;
- integration and management of the interfaces between processes;
- flow of information and process control across interfaces;
- service management processes.

Each certification audit will have an agreed scope with the auditor, which is then included on the certificate.

The certification audit process

A certification audit for ISO/IEC 20000 is similar to the audit involved when certifying to other management systems, such as ISO 9000 or ISO/IEC 27001. However, gaining certification to ISO 9000 does not automatically mean the service provider is certified to ISO/IEC 20000, even if both audits are carried out at the same time and by the same auditors.

An ISO 9000 audit checks for compliance with documented processes and PDCA requirements. A ISO/IEC 20000 audit includes checks for compliance with specific best practice service management processes.

The two standards can work together or each can be standalone. In practice and because of the specific nature of the ISO/IEC 20000 requirements, some service providers certified to ISO 9000 have to carry out additional service improvements to meet the requirements for introducing new or changed services and for the service management processes. The ISO/IEC 20000 and ISO 9000 certification schemes and certification audits are also separate, with separate audits and different certificates, even if both types of audits are done at the same time.

Certification schemes

Links to BS 15000

Many of the supporting activities and materials have been converted to ISO/IEC 20000 from BS 15000. This includes certification schemes.

The scope and applicability of ISO/IEC 20000:2005 is the same as for BS 15000:2002 with regards to certification schemes.

For service providers part-way through a programme after the publication of ISO/IEC 20000, the changes made during drafting of ISO/IEC 20000 had to be understood. These are described in BIP 0039, *The differences between BS 15000 and ISO/IEC 20000*.

Achieving BS 15000 was a contractual requirement of many commercial service providers, and the same may be the case for ISO/IEC 20000.

Available schemes

If a successful certification audit is carried out the service provider will be awarded a certificate, a process referred to as 'becoming certificated', or less commonly, 'being certified'.

The certificate awarded will include details of the scope of the audit and the credentials of the audit company and under what scheme they are registered to do the audits.

It is advisable to ensure that the audit company that is being considered as a candidate to do the certification is an 'accredited certification body'. A legitimate 'professional audit company' will have no problems about being required to prove their credentials, particularly for a service provider they have not worked for before.

Details that can be checked include those on their status as an accredited certification body, and which organization has in turn accredited them. They are also able to provide the details and track records of the individuals who will actually do the audit. It is essential for the individual auditors to understand IT service management, nor just for them to be experienced management system auditors or information security specialists. A prospective audit company may also be asked for references and case studies of similar audits, although the actual audit results are normally confidential.

Details of 'accreditation', 'accredited certification bodies', 'certification' etc are all described in Chapter 10.

There is an established certification scheme managed by itSMF, based on BS 15000. The first certificates under this scheme were awarded in February 2004.

This has been converted to an ISO/IEC 20000 scheme. Conversion of certification schemes has occurred for many other standards (e.g. the route for ISO 9000 and ISO/IEC 17799 and the ISO/IEC 27000 series).

What does 'self-certification' mean?

A service provider may claim compliance with ISO/IEC 20000 on the basis of 'self-certification'. This means they themselves have assessed their service management and believe that they meet requirements.
This is not the same as compliance under a certification audit,
i.e. self-certification is not certification. The difference is significant and is particularly important if ISO/IEC 20000 is being used as part of a procurement process, as described in Chapter 8.

CHAPTER 5

Scoping for service management

The scoping statement

Defining the scope of the service management processes for the planning and implementation of service management is one of the first requirements of ISO/IEC 20000. It is also necessary to agree the scope of a certification audit at an early stage. This is known as a scope statement.

The scope of the service management processes may be identical to the scope of the certification audit but service providers, at least for the first audit, may present a subset of their full service management activities for the audit. This is particularly common for large service providers who have the full range of processes for a series of different customers or locations and are using a staged approach to gaining certification for their whole enterprise.

Defining the scope for the planning and implementation of service management should not be treated as a separate or extra stage as a clearly defined scope is an important and integral part of service management and the PDCA cylce. The scope of an eventual audit should be agreed early in the planning stage before major service improvements are carried out. This will avoid wasting effort on preparing for an audit that cannot lead to ISO/IEC 20000 certification because the scope is inappropriate and does not meet the requirements.

The final decision on the acceptability of the scope rests with the auditors. The auditor should be presented with the proposed scope before the audit starts, so that any concerns can be resolved before the audit is carried out. The scope will also need to be re-checked for another audit.

The boundary of the service management processes in the audit scope can be based on parameters such as organization, location or service. Geographic boundaries may be defined by the service provider who may determine which locations are to be included in the audit scope. This decision may also be based on the location of the customer groups.

Organizational boundaries could be one or more customer groups for both internal and external service providers. Other parameters are possible under ISO/IEC 20000 requirements.

The processes that require full audit and those which require interfaces to be audited should be considered. Scoping, when there are complex supply chains, is illustrated in case studies later in this chapter. A key aspect of scoping for an audit is that every requirement in ISO/IEC 20000, i.e. every 'shall', has to be matched by evidence of best practice as defined in ISO/IEC 20000 (see definitions in Chapter 10).

One aspect that must be given careful consideration is how processes span organizational groups, including processes that may cross the organizational boundaries of complex supply chains.

Supply chains and audit scoping

Multiple suppliers

Many service providers are dependent on supply chains with complex customer-supplier relationships. A service provider may have many suppliers providing services. A service may be provided to many customers who themselves may also provide services. Each part of the supply chain contributes to the overall service delivered to the customer. This is illustrated by a relatively simple example of a supply chain, shown in Figure 6, which is from ISO/IEC 20000-1, 7.3.

In order to understand and define the scope of an audit, it is necessary to understand the existing supply chain for the delivery of the service and how that supply chain affects service management processes.

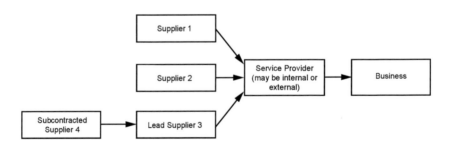

Figure 6 — Supply chains and service management

In the example in Figure 6, the service provider is the organization seeking certification under ISO/IEC 20000. Supplier 3 is a lead supplier, i.e. a supplier that takes the prime responsibility for delivering multiple services to the service provider, who in turn provides the service to the customer. In this example, only one subcontracted supplier is shown, but there may be several. This type of supply chain is a relatively simple example. It includes only one organization as a customer, wheareas service providers often have multiple customers.

A service provider may not be fully aware of the complexity of their supply chain until it is mapped out as part of the planning process for achieving ISO/IEC 20000. As well as the service provider, each of suppliers 1 to 3 in Figure 6 may be interested in achieving ISO/IEC 20000. Each organization should then consider the scope of their activities in order to decide if their services are appropriate for ISO/IEC 20000.

If one supplier in a supply chain is eligible for ISO/IEC 20000, it does not preclude another supplier in the supply chain from also being eligible. Nor is it necessary for each organization in a supply chain to achieve compliance with ISO/IEC 20000 for one to be eligible.

In many supply chains, more than one supplier will interface directly with the service provider so no one supplier is the lead supplier. A complex arrangement of suppliers may have happened gradually, or it may be the customer's policy to select multiple suppliers to get the most competitive service. This circumstance of dependency on suppliers, and in particular complex supply chains, may complicate the position of a service provider seeking certification to ISO/IEC 20000. This makes it even more important for a service provider to understand their position in a supply chain, and their dependencies on other organizations, for the service they deliver to their customer. It is essential for the respective roles of each organization to be understood, for the processes to be integrated and for all interfaces to be well managed.

Relationship management

ISO/IEC 20000 is written from the perspective of the service provider, i.e. the organization aiming to achieve ISO/IEC 20000 with interfaces to both suppliers and customers, so relationship management is split into business relationship management and supplier management.

- Business relationship management is the process followed by the service provider in dealing with its customers.

- Supplier management is the process followed by the service provider in dealing with suppliers when the service provider and supplier are part of a supply chain (see Figure 6).

The business relationship management process involves both parties agreeing details of the customer's business needs, service requirements, workload characteristics, roles and responsibilities, communications processes and customer satisfaction.

The supplier management process is vital because few individual service providers are responsible for every component of the service to a customer. The business relationship and supplier management process are described in more detail in BIP 0033, *Managing end-to-end service*.

Example: Simple scenario

The IT services department is the sole service provider of IT services in Company A. Company A is composed of four main business divisions: retail, sales and marketing, business operations, and finance and administration. IT services is part of finance and administration.

IT services have already implemented processes based on ITIL advice and guidance for their retail branches. During the coming year they plan to implement service management processes for back-office systems and aim to achieve compliance with ISO/IEC 20000 in the next year.

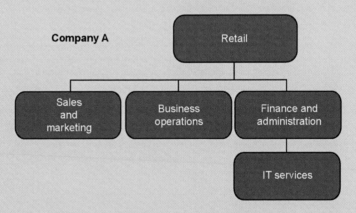

Figure 7– Organizational structure of Company A

May Company A seek certification for the IT services department?

Yes. If all the requirements are met, the ISO/IEC 20000 certificate would show the certificate had been awarded to Company A. The audit scoping statement with the certificate would clearly define that it was the IT services department that had been audited.

Example: Service desk outsourced

In this example, Company A have outsourced their service desk. This part of the service is now provided by Company B who provide first-line support (the service desk function) to Company A. Company A have direct line management responsibility for second- and third-line support teams (both of which are part of Company A).

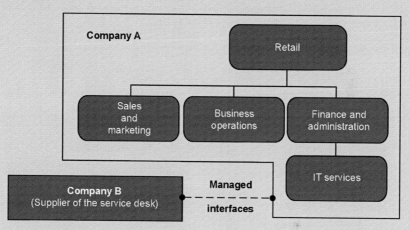

Figure 8 – Company A with a service desk provided by Company B

Will Company A's IT services department be able to seek ISO/IEC 20000 certification?

Despite not having the service desk within IT services, it may be able to achieve ISO/IEC 20000. This is because ISO/IEC 20000 is a process-based standard and makes no requirements for specific organizational units or functions to be in the scope of an audit, so having an outsourced service desk will not automatically prevent them achieving ISO/IEC 20000.

However, to achieve certification to ISO/IEC 20000, Company A's IT services department needs to show that it has retained management responsibility for all of the processes in the scope of ISO/IEC 20000. This is either by direct management responsibility for the process or by management of the process interfaces and supplier management. Company A's IT services department also needs to demonstrate that these processes are carried out within the organization (e.g. incident/problem management), even if the same processes cross the interface to the supplier, Company B, and are also carried out by Company B as part of providing the service desk function.

Example: Outsourcing to a supplier

Company A's IT services department is considering outsourcing application and infrastructure management Company B (see Figure 9). As part of this arrangement, Company A's IT services department is to completely outsource some of the processes, including problem and change management processes.

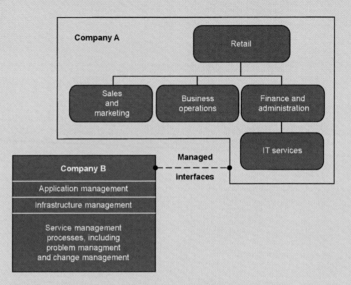

Figure 9 – Outsourced services and service management processes

Will Company A's IT service department still be able to seek ISO/IEC 20000 certification?

No, ISO/IEC 20000 would not be eligible for ISO/IEC20000 certification as they cannot demonstrate compliance with all the requirements (the 'shalls') and it is not an appropriate standard for Company A because it will no longer be responsible for the management of all ISO/IEC 20000 processes, such as problem management and parts of the PDCA cycle. As a result it can demonstrate neither direct nor indirect control of every ISO/IEC 20000 requirement.

However, although a ISO/IEC 20000 certification audit would not meet the requirements for scoping, there are other benefits to be gained from aiming in principle for the standard specified in ISO/IEC 20000. Company A will find ISO/IEC 20000 useful for assessments of their processes and those processes performed by their supplier. Company A may also decide that Company B needs to achieve certification to ISO/IEC 20000 to protect the service.

Frequently Asked Questions

What evidence is required for the management of interfaces?

Using Figure 8 as an example, there must be evidence that the process interfaces to the outsourced service desk are defined and managed. In this particular case study, the management of Company A's IT services department needs to define and manage incident management to a high standard. The interfaces should be defined in such a way to ensure that:

- all incidents for the defined services and infrastructure are recorded;

- incident information is available for use by all those that require it, not just those involved in the incident management process;

- procedures to manage the impact of service incidents are coordinated between the service desk supplier, Company B, and the service provider, Company A;

- the procedures that define the recording, prioritization, business impact, classification, updating, escalation, resolution and formal closure of all incidents are aligned across organizational boundaries;

- Company A's customers are kept informed of the progress of their reported incident, by an agreed and understood process;

- all actions are recorded on the incident record;

- all staff involved in incident management (first-, second- and third-line support groups in this case study) have access to relevant information such as known errors, problem resolutions and the configuration management database.

Information and management reports from the service desk provided by Company B need to be available to the second- and third-line support groups as service management cannot be effective without this. Other examples might require different interfaces to be defined and managed, e.g. outsourced continuity management. This is described in more detail in BIP 0038, *Integrated service management.*

For financial reasons an organization is split across several companies and is owned and managed by a single umbrella company. Can the separate companies share a ISO/IEC 20000 certificate?

Separate companies cannot share a certificate. This is the case even if the companies are all owned by the same single umbrella company. Certificates for standards such as ISO/IEC 20000 can only be awarded to a single legal entity. However, the umbrella company may be eligible for a certificate with a suitably detailed scoping statement. This is also the case with other management system standards, such as ISO 9000.

Does that mean the whole organization has to be audited, including all the separate companies managed by the umbrella company?

No, as long as the agreed scope includes all parts of ISO/IEC 20000 then only those parts of the organization need to be audited. This is quite common, especially with very large organizations. This example, of multiple companies all owned by the same umbrella company, is similar to a supply chain involving several suppliers.

What does each company have to do if they each wish to have their own ISO/IEC 20000 certificate?

Each company would have to be audited separately and each would have to meet the requirements. This might mean one of the companies was unable to meet the scoping requirements of ISO/IEC 20000. It might also mean one company might not pass the audit, even if the others did. Each company that does pass an audit will have a separate certificate defining the scope of their audit.

An organization does not have all of its processes in place, although the ones which do exist have been implemented to a high standard. Can they become part-certified?

No, they may not. Although it is not compulsory for the whole of an organization to be on the scope of an audit, all processes must be in the scope and all requirements contained in ISO/IEC 20000 are compulsory. Part-certification for just some of the processes is not possible.

You cannot exclude compulsory requirements by deciding they are not appropriate for your organization.

CHAPTER 6

Building the business case for ISO/IEC 20000

IT managers face increasing challenges. While maintaining flat or decreasing budgets and headcount, many managers are asked to improve service levels and enhance security while also justifying expenditure. For many of these managers achieving ISO/IEC 20000 will bring the benefits of improved services, more efficient service management processes, enhanced security and the ability to better understand costs. These improvements will make it easier to justify expenditure for any changes required in order to achieve ISO/IEC 20000.

The basis of the BS 15000 requirements, and now the ISO/IEC 20000 requirements, is that the best practices needed to achieve the standard actually improve efficiency and effectiveness and should not simply add a layer of bureaucracy. By reduced defects and risks most organizations should find that they have reduced their operating costs overall, with a strong shift towards more resources being used proactively and less reactively. The costs of service improvement will be directly linked to how much work is required, and for those that manage services badly the costs will be much higher, but also the benefits will be much greater when compared relatively to earlier circumstances.

For most service providers the cost of improving the service management processes will be the majority of the total costs of achieving ISO/IEC 20000. The costs of the actual certification audit are usually much smaller. Only service providers who are already operating with best practice service management will find the reverse is the case, i.e. that the costs of the actual audit are much greater than any remaining improvements required.

For any service provider the total costs of service improvements and the costs of an ISO/IEC 20000 audit should be outweighed by the benefits of the improvements. Costs will also continue to be incurred in order to retain this standard of service management, but again the overall benefits should outweigh the overall costs.

Initial decisions

Aiming for ISO/IEC 20000 is a significant decision for most organizations. Even a service provider with a high standard of service management may find that they have some gaps and weaknesses. Some service providers may decide to use ISO/IEC 20000 as a long-term goal because they recognize that they need to make significant improvements in their services and the way they deliver them. To make the most appropriate decision for their organization, management need to be clear on a number of key issues and make a number of key decisions before initiating a business case (such as in Checklist 1).

How long will it take, how much will it cost?

An important part of the decision making process is for a service provider to understand where it is starting from and what changes it will have to make. All service providers start from a different position and customer requirements may vary widely. The time and cost depends upon a variety of factors, such as the:

- scale and scope of the service provider's processes to be audited;
- existing quality of the processes;
- level and quality of documentation and records;
- understanding and training of staff;
- willingness of staff to change the way they work;
- management commitment;
- scale and nature of conflicting priorities;
- alignment with other initiatives;
- the advantage of phasing improvements and how this might be achieved.

Checklist 1: Key issues/decisions
Will ISO/IEC 20000 contribute to business objectives? Does the service provider need to make service improvements and, therefore, establish suitable goals for this?
Is there a direct or indirect commercial benefit from being able to prove achievement of ISO/IEC 20000?
What is the scope and scale of any required service improvements? Do they understand the requirements? Do they know what gaps and weaknesses there are and how these should be resolved?
What is the scope for a ISO/IEC 20000 audit? If they have services provided by external suppliers, does the service provider control the interfaces between themselves and those other suppliers?
Is the cost of achieving ISO/IEC 20000 justified? Will service improvements bring benefits that outweigh the costs of improvements and the cost of the actual audit?
What are the indicators of good performance? Does the service provider understand the requirements of ISO/IEC 20000 and of their customers?
What are the risks of not achieving the defined objectives? Might the staff involved be seriously demoralized if the service provider has to make major improvements over an extended period of time?
How does the service provider compare to others? Do they understand best practices and the lessons that can be learnt by assessing what others have achieved?

What makes a successful business case?

A successful business case will meet the following criteria.

- It is realistic and therefore trusted, i.e. it does not establish unrealistic timescales or costs that are too low for service improvements to be made.

- It provides the information that decision makers and planners need, i.e. objective and specific details of the current situation and the scale and nature of changes required.

- It predicts what will happen using sensible measures, i.e. it is based on objective data and opinions, with clarity on any assumptions using measures that relate to the interests of the customer and service provider.

All three are important but unless it is realistic and trusted it will not be accepted. Checklist 2 provides some examples of business case requirements.

Checklist 2: Business case requirements
An easily understood summary.
A real problem solved or a real benefit gained from implementation of ISO/IEC 20000.
Clarity on how it relates to the organization's business objectives.
An attractive but realistic payback time/return on investment.
Timing of individual cost and benefits across the period of the project i.e. return on investment at each stage.
Long-term benefits predicted for several years.
Sensible and clear timelines (initial service management changes may take years, not months).
Clarity on the subject, purpose and scope.
A proposed scope for the ISO/IEC 20000 audit which is sensible, i.e. not so small that it is unrepresentative of the service provider's service overall.
Language and terminology that does not require the reader to have specialist knowledge (i.e. using language the reader can relate to and taking care to avoid the use of jargon).
Numbers and not words making the business case easier to understand and taking up much less of the reader's time.
Suitable options and alternatives recommendations, including any important options considered and not included with reasons for exclusion.
All assumptions to be unambiguous and documented.
The key actions or decisions that are the subject of the business case to be easy to understand, with critical success factors included.
Clarity on the required decisions/permissions requested and on who will make what decisions.

A business case should be more like a management plan than a prediction. As with any plan, many things have to happen before the desired outcome can be reached. Therefore, the business case should describe the factors that can be managed or controlled during the project, e.g. the need for training, implementation of new service agreements with suppliers, and conflicts with other changes. Any risks must be quantified, particularly any that might halt progress towards achieving ISO/IEC 20000.

Sensitivity and risk analyses produce two kinds of information about uncertainties. They determine:

- **sensitivity:** which assumptions are most important in controlling overall results?

- **risks:** the likelihood of other outcomes instead of the ones predicted.

Many business cases are misleading because they leave out important benefits and costs. Readers will more readily accept business cases when there is no ambiguity about their value. Projected cost savings usually fall into this category, as the rationale for estimating them is understood, straightforward and is more easily defended. Omissions are therefore usually intangible benefits or costs that are hard to quantify, difficult to describe, but are still potentially large. For some service providers intangible costs and benefits may outweigh tangible costs and benefits. The writer of the business case may not understand them or underestimates them. For example, benefits like 'improved customer satisfaction' or 'enhanced market image' or 'better employee morale' also have value, but are harder to quantify than tangible benefits such as X% less incidents, so may be omitted as being somehow not quite 'real'.

A good business case contains a recommendations section that identifies all of the viable options. The case must include who needs to do what, by when, in order for the predicted results to be delivered. Typical topics that may be addressed in a business case are given in Table 5 as an illustration.

Table 5 – Preparing your business case

1. Management summary
Like any management summary this must be concise, cover the key points made in the body of the document and give the high level cost-benefits and risks of each option presented.

2. Background
The recent history of service management and other changes in your organization must not be ignored as they will influence the decision on a ISO/IEC 20000 business case. Memories of recent events, particularly those relating to major changes or serious problems with the service will determine the 'tone' of the business case. There will have been experiences that will influence whether a business case for ISO/IEC 20000 will be accepted or not, such as 'We put the service desk in place and the service is no better', 'Since we introduced change management we've not had any serious impact on the business from failed changes'.
History should not be ignored but instead built into the case to:
• explain success in order to justify 'more of the same';
• explain failures in order to justify a different approach.

3. Project description
Project name
A good project name is brief yet descriptive, presenting the reader with an image of what will be achieved, e.g. 'Benefits from ISO/IEC 20000' or 'ISO/IEC 20000 as a goal for service improvement'.
Project sponsors/stakeholders
The person(s) responsible for initiating and managing the implementation of ISO/IEC 20000 should be identified. The actual planned or proposed service management process owners, specified in ISO/IEC 20000, should also be identified as sponsors or stakeholders.
Asking senior managers in the customer organization to be sponsors or stakeholders may help if the customers are concerned about the changes, particularly if there have been failed initiatives before or there is scepticism about the benefits (see BIP 0031, *Why people matter*).

Table 5 – Preparing your business case (*continued*)

Start date and planned end dates
If the work is to be carried out in stages, the end dates may be a series of dates with each one representing a milestone. It may be necessary to establish dates to align with (or avoid) major business changes. The business case may actually position implementation of ISO/IEC 20000 as a milestone or precursor to other changes. If this is the case there should be a link to the Purpose/objectives.

4. Purpose/objectives
This answers the question 'Why are we doing this?'. The purpose and objectives are usually a mix of problems to be resolved and opportunities to be seized. ISO/IEC 20000 business cases will usually include the need to make services more cost-effective and more appropriate to a customer's needs. Both of these objectives should be quantified, i.e. How much more cost-effective? What is appropriate?

The business case should outline opportunities or problems that the project will address. Making service management 'better, cheaper, faster' may be the underlying purpose of any business case, but a good ISO/IEC 20000 business case positions certification as a means of gaining the expected benefits of service management improvements. It also quantifies 'better, cheaper, faster' by establishing realistic and measurable goals.

For example, the benefits might be summarized as any, or all, of the following.

- Reduction of the number of incidents and problems by X%, saving X% in direct support costs and X% in the customer's operating costs (from problem management).
- Improvement of the fix time for all calls logged by the service desk by X% saving X% in direct support costs and X% in the customer's costs (from incident management).
- Reduction of the frequency of major business problems affecting the customer's business activities from failed changes by X% (from change management).

Other objectives may be less tangible such as the following.

- Increased credibility of the customer's business activities leading to X% increase in business customer retention and X% growth in business customer retention.
- A foundation for business continuity (this means certification to ISO/IEC 20000 may lead to other new initiatives).

Table 5 – Preparing your business case (*continued*)

- Passing the next external audit (e.g. Food and Drug Administration (FDA)[6], financial audits, Sarbanes-Oxley[7], public sector 'best value' checks);
- Reducing by X% the corrective action required after the next audit.

When defining the objectives, identify the opportunities delivered or problems addressed by achieving compliance with ISO/IEC 20000. Quantify these and, if possible, express them in business terms as the required changes may have a fundamental impact on end users that rely on the service.

Examples of business benefits may include the following.

- Reducing the management overhead of time spent with unhappy business customers and handling complaints about the service.
- Delivering a new business product faster than the competition.
- The establishment of sound service management processes allowing for more focus on innovation and added value.

Benefits specific to IT services may include the following.

- Avoiding threatened cuts to the support budget by improving customer satisfaction.
- The supply chain, including third-party suppliers, is managed properly so that the end result is optimized.
- The benefits gained from processes being fully integrated with interfaces managed.
- Standard costs can be identified and employed more easily.
- With standard costs identified and consistent service delivery, budgeting and forecasting can be assessed more accurately allowing for more confident decision making.

If the objectives are not defined clearly in the business case, it is likely that the risks (and long-term benefits) have not been properly understood. Subsequently, they will not be managed properly during the project or taken into account in the cost-benefit calculations.

---

[6] The Food and Drug Administration (FDA) is a US body with regulations that impact organizations outside the US.

[7] Sarbanes-Oxley is US legislation requiring a high standard of probity in control of information, and in particular financial information. The requirements for parts of this are met by being able to demonstrate a high standard of service management process control and the ability to provide an audit trail of changes.

Table 5 – Preparing your business case (*continued*)

5. Scope of ISO/IEC 20000 audits

It is important to include the scope of the proposed ISO/IEC 20000 audit in the business case because it will influence the scope and scale of the ISO/IEC 20000 project. A draft scope statement will help this.

If the final scope of the ISO/IEC 20000 audit is wider than the service improvement scope then there is a strong risk that certification will not be achieved. The opposite is not true. Improvements may be made on a wider scale than the actual changes being audited, without putting certification at risk.

If the scope is too broad or open-ended then a service provider may invest a lot of time and money working towards a certification audit which could lead to a very long project with a high risk of failure. As described in Chapter 5, incorrect scoping can cause serious issues and so the proposed scope must be clear in the business case.

If the service management scope cannot be matched to a scope acceptable for ISO/IEC 20000, then ISO/IEC 20000 may be the wrong standard for your organization. An alternative, such as ISO 9000 or a maturity model, may be more suitable. Often a phased approach to ISO/IEC 20000 is based on increasing the scope of the audit (and re-audit) for ISO/IEC 20000, as described below.

Inclusions and exclusions

The scope should take into account the:

- organization(s) – what are the legal boundaries?
- functions – do the functions cover all the processes directly or indirectly?
- geography and location – does the scope cover all locations or just one small office?
- services – is it the service for one type of business activity or all services?
- customers/users – is it applicable to a type of customer/user or all customers/users? Are they internal or external?
- interfaces – are the interfaces between processes clear, understood, integrated and managed?
- suppliers – is the supply chain understood and managed effectively?

Table 5 – Preparing your business case (*continued*)

Phasing
Phased increases in scope may also be advisable, i.e. only some services, locations or customers at first and then more phased in later. Even if the intention is to proceed with incremental increases in the scope, each audit stage must cover a scope that is acceptable for a ISO/IEC 20000 certification audit.

6. Project scope
Service improvements
The scope could, for example, describe the changes/improvements required to: • establish problem management; • improve incident management; • extend configuration management; • consolidate change management processes; • establish business relationship processes.   Any other projects that will influence service management need to be referred to and allowed for in the planning. For example, roll out of a new standard desktop or a major business change may cause clashes that prevent the ISO/IEC 20000 project progressing to the agreed timetable. The risks may be considered to be too high and skilled staff may be stretched too thin.   Conversely, service management improvements may be needed in order to prepare for other initiatives, such as a major business change, so it becomes a prerequisite before the major change can be implemented. For example, it might be viewed that business continuity, however important, cannot work until service management is of a high standard. The scale of implementation for a new service may be so large that it will only be manageable with rigorous service management processes already established, such as configuration, change and release management.

Table 5 – Preparing your business case (*continued*)

7. Costs and benefits
Each company will have rules on how cost-benefits are to be scoped and calculated. For example, any office refurbishments required for a ISO/IEC 20000 project may be handled as part of 'business as usual' costs (i.e. they need to happen anyway) and therefore will not influence the ISO/IEC 20000 business case. In contrast, the service provider may decide that automation is the simplest way of making some of the required improvements and may decide to include the costs of purchase and implementation in the costs of the cost-benefit, even though ISO/IEC 20000 includes no requirement for automation.
Tangible costs: Capital costs
These are costs where an asset is gained even if it is used only for the duration of the ISO/IEC 20000 project. These items are normally depreciated over a fixed term and the service provider's rules on depreciation need to be considered. Typical capital costs include: <ul><li>hardware;</li><li>software;</li><li>telecommunications;</li><li>implementation costs;</li><li>fixtures and fittings.</li></ul>
Recurring/revenue costs
Recurring/revenue costs are the ones you can expect to pay regularly in future years, such as: <ul><li>salaries;</li><li>maintenance for hardware;</li><li>software upgrades;</li><li>rentals/leases;</li><li>travel;</li><li>training.</li></ul>
Non-recurring costs
This type of cost is one incurred for the project but which leaves no tangible financial assets. Depending on the specific item and on your organization's financial rules this may be capital or revenue funded.

Table 5 – Preparing your business case (*continued*)

Examples of non-recurring costs include:

- human resources/costs of staff involved in the project;
- facility upgrades;
- external advisors for a pre-audit review or benchmarking;
- office accommodation used during service improvements and auditing;
- the cost of the audit.

Risks/intangible costs

Management of risk is one of the key costs in any business change, such as certifying against ISO/IEC 20000. This includes wide-ranging issues such as:

- distraction from other changes to the detriment of the service;
- conflicts on resources, i.e. too few staff to do anything properly;
- short-term disruption on the service and customers' business.

Benefits

Intangible benefits are important and more difficult to quantify than tangible benefits. In addition to external marketing and commercial benefits (e.g. a commercial supplier winning more business), ISO/IEC 20000 provides a recognized and 'tried and tested' management system which allows a service provider to plan, manage, deliver, monitor, report, review and improve its services. ISO/IEC 20000 not only looks at operational aspects of the service but also focuses on the business controls, covering associated risks, finances, resources and capabilities, providing a proper infrastructure to enable a traditional PDCA cycle to be implemented and managed.

Productivity gains

The benefits of productivity gains are wide ranging and can include the following.

- Each process is more efficient so it is faster and therefore potentially cheaper.
- Problems are avoided so workload is reduced.
- Staff take more pride in their job, become enthusiastic and work more productively.
- Stable workforce reduces the risk of high turnover and loss of specialist skills.
- Service is improved overall.
- The same service will be cheaper.

Table 5 – Preparing your business case (*continued*)

These benefits arise from improvements in service management, e.g. improved incident management means the service is returned to normal faster, impacting the customer less. Problem management prevents the service being interrupted, while change management reduces the risk of failed changes. A reduction in failed changes in turn reduces the numbers incidents and problems, so that the customer's business activities are not impacted. Many other similar benefits arise from service management process improvements, including the transition from a predominantly reactive to a predominantly proactive organization.

People prefer to work for a successful organization and successful service management processes create an atmosphere where staff are more motivated and productive, customers are happier and overheads, such as escalations and complaint handling, are reduced. Training and succession planning becomes easier as staff are following best practice processes and there is clarity on who does what. There will be an overall reduction in the effort required to deliver the service and in the overall cost.

Process changes

Many of the features of sub-standard service management processes, such as variations in processes, originate when service management is being implemented in isolation or when processes evolve over time. The solution to this is process changes, although staff (or customers) may resist the new or improved processes. Typical benefits from process changes include:

- processes becoming more transparent to all support staff and users;
- process utilization and compliance being monitored and measured more easily;
- services being delivered at a lower risk;
- services being more flexible and responsive;
- easier workload management, allowing optimization of the process from continuing improvements in efficiency;
- end users being able to do something for the first time, e.g. guarantee a deliverable by a stated time and be sure it will be achieved (resulting in a more reliable and predictable service);
- Sarbanes-Oxley type requirements being met;
- meeting public sector 'best value' requirements.

Table 5 – Preparing your business case (*continued*)

Improved customer satisfaction

A low standard of service is a cause of complaint, increased management overheads and lost business opportunity for the customers reliant on the service provider's service. ISO/IEC 20000 can provide a framework for the changes to occur, which can also provide the benefit of a common goal that will be supported by the staff affected. Some of the less tangible benefits arising from this include:

- a more positive change in attitude;
- less overheads caused by escalations;
- less overheads caused by complaints;
- a belief that the service provider can be trusted;
- protection of the service provider's budgets against cuts made by unhappy customers.

Competitive advantage

Commercial service providers may consider competitive advantage to be the most important aspect of achieving ISO/IEC 20000. However, there are many forms of competitive advantage. For example, a fast, cheaper, improved service will give the customers advantages. In-house service providers will be motivated to improve services to ensure that they retain the customer's business, avoiding a loss of scale from a multiple supplier arrangement that erodes economies of scale.

Some key advantages are:

- 'first mover advantage', i.e. the first organization to move into a new area of operation or provide a completely new product;
- becoming more competitive;
- retaining customers;
- attracting new customers.

8. Recommendations

These should include each realistic option for ISO/IEC 20000. As a rule of thumb, a maximum of four recommendations are advisable or the differences between each option will be too small to be of importance and simply confuse the decision making process. For example, two or three of the following options could be used as in a ISO/IEC 20000 case.

Table 5 – Preparing your business case (*continued*)

Option	Comments
Do nothing	An option that has to be considered during planning, even though doing nothing is not normally beneficial. In the short term doing nothing may allow there to be a period of stability, which can in itself bring about some improvements as people and processes settle into a routine. In the medium and long term doing nothing may lead to a degradation in the effectiveness of the processes as they stagnate
Adopt ISO/IEC 20000 as a quality goal, stopping short of ISO/IEC 20000 certification audit	This is either compliance with ISO/IEC 20000 or carrying out an audit that is not a certification audit
Phased improvements with ISO/IEC 20000 certification audits repeated for a wider scope each time	An approach that is common for many management system standards like ISO/IEC 20000
Service improvements in phases with the actual certification audit carried out for all services at the end	It is difficult for the whole of a large organization to achieve ISO/IEC 20000 in this way. It potentially takes so long that the pace of the initiative is lost
Go for ISO/IEC 20000 linked to ISO 9000	ISO/IEC 20000 may be linked to a more specialist standard, a generic quality standard ISO 9000 or a maturity/capability model .

Each option must be accompanied by a quantified breakdown of costs, benefits, risks, dependencies, success criteria and a high level plan that will be unique to your organization. Tangible costs, intangible costs and benefits must be covered with all assumptions described.

For ISO/IEC 20000, the investments are in the cost of the service management improvements, the cost of the self-assessment and/or pre-audit reviews and the cost of the actual audit itself. The benefits are improved services, with less tangible benefits in the form of improved staff morale and greater credibility as a service provider.

9. Generic plan

A Gantt chart showing the key tasks, milestones and dependencies should be included.

Accountancy terms and cost-benefits calculations

BIP 0034, Finance for service managers covers aspects of financial management as well as the requirements and recommendations in ISO/IEC 20000. Each organization has rules about how cost-benefits are handled and the business case needs to reflect this. Consult your organization's finance department when you start to build the business case. Also look at previous business cases, successful and unsuccessful, in order to gain an understanding of what is required of your ISO/IEC 20000 business case. Most organizations involve their finance department in building and assessing business cases, and so you will not be required to become an accountancy expert in order to produce the case. However, the following cost-benefit measures are commonly used by many organizations.

Return on investment (ROI)

The business benefit (i.e. the return) of an investment. It is calculated as a percentage difference between benefits and costs divided by the total investment. In ISO/IEC 20000 terms it is the benefits (or cost savings) arising from service management improvements divided by the cost of the improvements over a period of time. The timescale needs to be over several years even though some of the benefits may deliver within weeks.

Payback period

The time it takes for an investment to pay for itself, i.e. recovery of the original investment. Like the ROI, payback is insensitive to the economic life of a ISO/IEC 20000 project and assumes constant benefits (cash inflows). The payback method does not consider cash flow beyond the payback time.

Chapter 7

Preparing for an audit

What will the auditor expect to see?

ISO/IEC 20000-1 is a specification, therefore the auditor will expect to see evidence that all of the requirements contained in ISO/IEC 20000-1 have been met. For example, ISO/IEC 20000-1, clause 3.1 states:

'Management shall establish the service management policy, objectives and plans.'

The use of 'shall' in a specification indicates a compulsory requirement that the service provider has to meet in order to comply with the standard. This is a requirement of the standard and not a legal or statutory requirement. (See Chapter 10 for an explanation of terms used in international standards and certification schemes.)

If the service provider aims to meet the requirement in clause 3.1, it is compulsory that the top/executive management establishes a management policy, objectives and plans. The auditor will check that this has been completed effectively.

All requirements have to be in the scope of the audit. Service providers who do not meet all requirements will not be able to achieve ISO/IEC 20000. As described in Chapter 5, clarity in the scoping of the audit is especially important where there are complex supply chains.

BIP 0015 – the self-assessment workbook

There are very few service providers whose service management processes cannot be improved in order to achieve compliance with ISO/IEC 20000. In reality, one of the benefits of ISO/IEC 20000 is that it gives a benchmark for service improvement programmes to aim for. Experience to date indicates that service providers can carry out useful assessments of their own processes before deciding whether to aim for ISO/IEC 20000. Many have used BIP 0015, *IT service management – Self-assessment workbook,* for this purpose, particularly in the early stages of a programme to improve processes.

Experience has also shown that it is harder to be objective about something you are involved with or responsible for on a day-to-day basis, even with the aid of BIP 0015. Those carrying out the assessment also may have reservations about finding faults in the work of their colleagues. An assessment can be demoralizing if handled tactlessly, with people becoming unwilling to try to improve the processes because they feel they are so far short of meeting the requirements.

In addition, an inexperienced assessor may not have the breadth of experience to carry out the assessment properly or may not be able to distinguish the differences between requirements, recommendations and informative text (see Appendix A).

Service providers have usually found it helpful to have someone who is not involved with the process on a day-to-day basis to carry out a pre-audit assessement. This can range from each process owner or manager assessing a process they do not themselves have close involvement with (e.g. a change manager assessing the business relationship management process) through to a formal pre-audit assessment by independent specialists in service management.

 Example: The stages of a pre-audit assessment

Stage 1 – Background and review of documentation

The following documents should be available for review at the start of the assessment:

- service management policies and plans;
- processes and procedures within the scope of ISO/IEC 20000;
- service level agreements (and supporting agreements and contracts);
- records required by the standard (change records, service reports, checklists, etc.);
- organizational structure charts;
- supply chain mapping showing suppliers, the service provider and the customers, including their locations
- proposed scope for the audit.

The first four items are required for preliminary checks (e.g. is the service provider far short or close to ISO/IEC 20000 requirements? Audit scope, the last item, is used to plan the detailed assessment and should have been the subject to preliminary discussions before major service improvements.

Stage 2 – Detailed assessment

Stage 2 should involve a number of activities, designed to fill in the gaps in the information provided in advance of the pre-audit review. This stage also gives the opportunity for potential issues to be progressed and understood in more detail. Once there is an understanding of the service provider's capabilities, an action plan for outstanding improvements can be agreed. It is particularly important that responsibilities for short-term and long-term improvements are well understood. The detailed assessment may cover:

- presentations;
- tours of the facilities;
- face-to-face meetings;
- ISO/IEC 20000 project team meetings;
- use of BIP 0015, *IT service management – Self-assessment workbook*;
- discussions to clarify responsibilities (See BIP 0031, *Why people matter*);
- feedback on findings and recommended options from the independent reviewers.

Stage 3 – Post visit

Following the site visit, a project brief for achieving compliance with ISO/IEC 20000 should be produced. This could include:

- detailed analysis of the service provider's strengths and weaknesses compared to ISO/IEC 20000;
- a detailed plan of what steps are now required and how these steps can be integrated in an improvement programme;
- any supplementary comments on potential improvements that may not be required to achieve ISO/IEC 20000 but which may still be helpful to the service provider (e.g. organizational or charging issues);
- any weaknesses that may undermine the ability of the service provider to meet the ISO/IEC 20000 requirements.

Service improvements

The preparation for the audit may include extensive improvements to the service management processes, their integration and their overall management, including the PDCA components. A key element of this is the top-down management approach and establishment of policies.

The plan

The size, complexity and distribution of the customer's and service provider's businesses are among the factors that should be input into a plan. Cost-benefits must also be included.

The stages in ISO/IEC 20000 project can be summarized as:

- gap analysis or pre-audit assessment;

- identify process owners for:

  a) management responsibilities, including PDCA components;

  b) service management overall;

  c) each of the 13 service management processes;

- define and document missing or inadequate:

  a) policies;

  b) processes;

  c) procedures;

- establish changes to roles and responsibilities (See BIP 0031, *Why people matter*);

- establish any organizational changes;

- implement process changes, normally in phases;

- review and fine-tune changes.

The role of policies

Agreeing the formal policies is one of the benefits of aiming for compliance with ISO/IEC 20000. When policies have been defined they should be linked to processes and procedures, in a logical hierarchy, as shown in Figure 10. Figure 10 illustrates a very simple hierarchy with one process dependent on one policy and one procedure dependent on one process. In reality the service provider may chose to have a set of policies, rather than a single large service management policy in the scope of ISO/IEC 20000. Each policy may have several dependent processes. This logical hierarchy links the intentions of a service provider to what it actually does on a day to day basis.

Service providers that have previously written formal policies for security or business continuity reasons only will find they benefit from having a full set of policies, linked to processes which are in turn linked to procedures.

When properly completed, this should align business needs, the objectives of each process and the workplace practices. Establishing formal policies for the first time may highlight that there has been a gap between business needs and service management practices.

Example policies

These policies are examples based on real policies from real service providers, but are not necessarily relevant or appropriate for all service providers.

Example: Service management policy

The Company's information systems and services will be designed, delivered and maintained under best practice processes and procedures, as specified by ISO/IEC 20000. This includes interfaces to processes outside the direct control of the Company.

The service management policies, processes and procedures provide the foundation for assessing potential suppliers of information services to the Company.

Staff will be trained to ensure competency and appropriate support. Review processes will be defined to ensure compliance. The service management processes will also define roles and responsibilities as the basis of training and competency.

Metrics will be defined to measure the quality of information services processes and provide a basis for benchmarking against other leading companies in regulated industries. These metrics will also be used to ensure that the defined standards are maintained and to trigger remedial action, where necessary.

The processes and procedures will be regularly reviewed and enhanced to incorporate innovations and improvements in best practice.

Example: Change management policy

All parts of the Company must follow the standard procedures for change management. All changes to the operational service must be processed by the standard change management process. In the case of services provided by suppliers, the contract terms affecting the change management process must have the agreement of the Company's change management process owner. The standard procedures for underpinning the change management process include a provision for discussion and evaluation with the relevant departments and any change must not be implemented until clearance is given by the change manager and service delivery manager. Procedures will also include monitoring and reviewing the effects of change and each department will assist with this process.

The assessment itself

As described in Chapter 4, *Compliance and certification audits*, there are professional audit companies who are able to carry out a certification audit both in and outside of the UK. The audit company will estimate the cost of the audit based on an understanding of the scale, scope and nature of the service provider's services and customer base. The ability to demonstrate capability to do audits for other management system standards (such as ISO 9000) does not automatically mean there will be the capability in auditing service management processes that is required for an ISO/IEC 20000 audit.

Conversely, an understanding of service management, however great, is not adequate to do an ISO/IEC 20000 audit, as it is equally important that the audit company and auditor understand how to audit management system requirements, including how the PDCA cycle interfaces with service management and what is required for integration of processes.

It is particularly important for an auditor to understand that ISO/IEC 20000 is fundamentally about 'doing not documenting'.

Areas that the auditor will check include the following.

- If the service is reliant on a complex chain of suppliers, the auditor will expect to see clear evidence of how the interfaces are managed, not just the supplier management process, but any process where there is an interaction with suppliers and lead suppliers.

- The auditor will expect to see how all interfaces to customers are managed, not only the business relationship management process, but also any of the other processes where there is an interface with the customers or users.

- Information flows are important in ISO/IEC 20000 and the auditor will expect to see more than just service reports. The auditor will want to see how information is actually used within each process and how it flows across interfaces, including those across supplier-service provider-customer interfaces.

- If there are many different locations used to provide the service, or the customers are based at many different locations and they are all in the scope of the audit, the auditors will make a decision on whether each location will be audited or whether a few will be chosen as a representative sample. The decision will normally be made during the assessment and is subject to change.

- The auditor will expect to see a policy or a series of policies that relate to each of the processes and procedures in the scope.

- The documentation should be concise, easy to understand, widely available and under good control. It should also reflect reality and be used for staff training.

Audit evidence

Documentary evidence

During an assessment or an actual certification audit, it will be necessary to provide documentary evidence against each of the requirements in ISO/IEC 20000. One of the advantages of assessing what evidence will be required for the audit is that there will be a sounder basis for the understanding of the requirements in the early planning stage.

Is the evidence something just for the audit?

The evidence required consists of the documents and records that are required anyway for good service management, i.e. it is not correct to produce documents simply to provide evidence for an audit.

A professional auditor would be alert to this and is likely to treat this as a fault in the processes.

'Doing not documenting'

It is important that those involved strike a balance between too little (leading to inconsistency in approach) and too much (leading to excessively bureaucratic processes). This decision should take into account that, although documentation is part of good service management, meeting the requirements of ISO/IEC 20000 is about 'doing not documenting'. Senior management are responsible for ensuring that documents and records are available for an audit.

Pitfalls to avoid

One of the pitfalls is that production of documentation can be seen as more important than changing how people work (i.e. documenting, not doing). Aiming for ISO/IEC 20000 should not involve a spree of mass document.

Excessive documentation built up over time is generally an indicator of ad hoc initiatives and that the PDCA requirements are being followed badly. There may be little or no logical structure to how the documents relate and with little or no commonality to format and style or level of detail. Typically, the first documents will be work instructions or procedures written because an individual's day-to-day activities have never been documented. This may later extend to the mapping of a process when it has been decided that improvements are needed. Processes may be described without process maps and may be combined with (or confused with) procedures.

Documents often contain a high proportion of irrelevant detail, e.g. justification of why a particular procedure is in place or the history of how it was implemented. This has no place or purpose in good documents.

Many service providers produce documents as the result of localized initiatives so that procedures are written in isolation of the logical relationship between policy, process, procedures and plans that is required by ISO/IEC 20000.

Many service management documents are defective because they are too long, not because they are too short.

Other common pitfalls are that the scope of each document and the relationship between documents is unclear. Interfaces may not be documented and even if the processes have been integrated, the integration may not be documented. The next chapter describes how to avoid this.

CHAPTER 8

Documents and records

Introduction

This chapter describes the ISO/IEC 20000 requirements and recommendations for documents and records. It is important to understand this aspect of the standard well before planning to achieve ISO/IEC 20000.

 Definitions: Document and record

'Document' is used to describe information and its supporting medium. Information is in readable form and may include computer data. It is evidence of the service provider's intentions with regards to service management. Examples include policy statements, plans, processes, procedures, service level agreements and contracts.

'Record' is used to describe document stating results achieved or providing evidence of activities performed. Records function as evidence of activities, rather than evidence of intentions. Examples include audit reports, requests for change, incident reports, individual training records and invoices.

'Doing not documenting'

Achieving ISO/IEC 20000 is not about a large volume of documents produced only to satisfy an auditor. It is about useful and fit-for-purpose documents and records. These are most successful if they are concise, are easy to retrieve and manage and do not overlap or conflict with other documents and records. The following example illustrates the issues that can arise from too much documentation.

Example: Issues with too much documentation

A service provider assessed its service management capability. The biggest issue was quality and quantity of documents:

- there were many instances of errors and out-of-date documents.

- procedures were in very long documents;

- procedures duplicated information that staff learned on courses;

- process and procedure were treated as interchangeable documents;

- staff were unclear which document to use;

- staff could not understand the logic of the document index;

- the search facility produces unexpected documents;

A manager was allocated responsibility for document management, a role equivalent to a process owner. The manager adopted a ruthless approach, giving three weeks notice that all documents, except those that related to security, service continuity and staff employment would be archived off site, unless a good case was made for retention of a specific document. Few documents fell into this category, the rare exceptions being documents about the topology of the infrastructure.

The manager agreed a new document library structure, document management policies, processes and procedures and templates. Some existing documents were reused but reduced in length so that policies were less than one page, and processes a maximum of two pages. The document control information was reduced to a single page at the end. All documents were placed under the control of a web-enabled document indexing and search facility.

Documents were much easier to write and change and staff were trained in writing, reviewing and using documents.

Key point:

Staff were able to locate information that they needed quickly and it was far more useful. This encouraged them to adopt a consistent approach to their work, which improved the service management.

The role of documents and records

Although ISO/IEC 20000 is about 'doing not documenting', documents and records do make an important contribution to service management. They represent the service provider's 'organizational memory' and provide explicit, codified knowledge, in contrast to the tacit knowledge in people's heads. Documents and records are evidence of the certainty, repeatability and durability of practice and knowledge.

Documents bring many benefits to the service provider, including:

- clarity of understanding;

- easier and better communications;

- easier coordination;

- collaboration and knowledge sharing;

- control.

Documents facilitate repeatability, traceability and collaborative working across organizational and functional interfaces.

Records provide evidence of systematic and effective planning, operation and control of service management. Records relating to staff development and competence must also be maintained.

Types of documents and records

Each service provider determines the document and record types required under their particular circumstances. Valid differences that must be recognized and accommodated include:

- size of service provider's organization;

- number and competence of the service provider's staff;

- range, nature and scale of services;

- scale and complexity of the supported infrastructure;

- complexity of processes and of process interfaces;

- supplier services relied on by the service provider.

- the nature of the customer's business activities;

- number and competence of users;

- legal and regulatory requirements;

There are broad categories of documents that apply to most service providers, such as classification by purpose, including:

- description of the management system and how it applies to the service management plan;

- 'how to', e.g. processes, procedures that must be performed consistently;

- 'what to do' – procedures that must be performed consistently;

- statement of requirements;

- definition of commitments between the service provider, customer and any suppliers.

Records can be classified by the evidence they provide, including:

- results achieved;

- activities performed;

- traceability and verification;

- preventive action;

- corrective action;

- improvements made.

Media and format

The choice of media and format must ensure that documents and records are secure but accessible. For example, if a network diagram is developed in a drawing package, staff using the information must have easy access to the diagram, and this normally requires access to the package used to produce it.

Media may be hard copy, electronic or a combination of the two. Many service providers publish electronically, with access via an intranet or shared access file structure. The format varies according to the choice of media and type of document or record.

Controls

Evidence of control

An auditor will expect to see evidence of documents having been under control for a period of time before the audit in order to detect weaknesses in the controls, or failures to comply with the controls.

Controls typically include:

- use of templates;
- unique document identification, registration and version cotnrol;
- identification, registration and control of external documents;
- change management of documents;
- tracking of document status and changes to status;
- review and approval of documents prior to issue or re-issue;
- security from the use of backup sources;
- protection against damage or unauthorized access;
- media and format giving appropriate access and ease of use;
- policy, process and procedure on withdrawal, archiving and disposal of old versions.

There also needs to be control over the readability of documents by the use of simple language.

Document and record life cycle

The service provider is required to control documents and records and define responsibilities covering the document lifecycle stages:

- creation;
- review;
- approval;
- maintenance;
- control;
- disposal.

Responsibilities must also be defined for each stage of the document life cycle. It is normally useful to include responsibility matrices with the details of what is to be done at each stage. This clarity assists with sensible distribution of tasks, workload, accountability and responsibility. It also enables the identification of potential clashes within the life cycle stages that may arise if it is unclear who would be doing what and when they would be doing it. For example, it is normally considered bad practice for the person who creates a document to also review it and the person who reviews it is not normally the person who authorizes it.

Usually someone who does not get involved in document creation is given responsibility for their control, perhaps with the job title 'Document Librarian'. Once document control is established, this may not be a full-time role, even for a large service provider with many documents.

Examples of responsibility matrices covering the life cycle of documents and records are given in Tables 6 and 7. Table 6 represents each stage of the document and record life cycle. Table 7 shows only the approval stage, expanded to show more detail.

Configuration and change management

ISO/IEC 20000-1, 9 includes requirements that documents on service or infrastructure are managed by the change and configuration management processes as described in BIP 0035, *Enabling change*.

Many service providers find it beneficial for all documents and records to be configuration items and to be managed in this way.

The service management framework

To control documents it is necessary to understand the relationships between them so the implications of change to one of them can be fully understood.

A service management framework, such as that shown in Figure 10, can illustrate the relationships. For example:

- training documents – may be related to the policy, process, procedure for a process;

- service catalogue – describes overall customer services that are partially provided under contracts with suppliers.

A service provider's own framework may be more complex than the illustration in Figure 10, particularly if the framework shows links to individual documents and not just document types.

When the service management plans are changed, tracking of achievements against objectives needs to change as well. Changes will normally ripple through and impact individual documents and records. For example, if a change to the service management plan is related to a specific service, such as a payroll service, then there may also be updates to the service level agreement for that service.

Table 6 – Responsibility matrix for a document and record life cycle

Process: incident management	Accountable	Responsible	Consulted	Informed
	Creation	Senior responsible owner	Service manager	Process owners
Support staff	Document librarian		Review	Incident management process owner
All process owners	Support staff	Document librarian		
Approval	**Senior responsible owner**	**Incident management Process owner**	**Service improvement manager**	**Document librarian**
Maintenance	Incident management process owner	Service improvement manager	Other process owners	Document librarian
Control	Senior responsible owner	Document librarian	—	All staff and process managers
Disposal	Senior responsible owner	Document librarian	Other process owners	All staff and process managers

Table 7 – Responsibility matrix for the Approval stage

Approval stage	Accountable	Responsible	Consulted	Informed
Confirm purpose/quality criteria	Senior responsible owner	Senior responsible owner	Incident management process owner	Document librarian
Compare to planned contents	Incident management process owner	Service improvement manager	-	-
Assess quality/fit for purpose	Incident management process owner	Service improvement manager	All process owners	-
Accept or reject	Senior responsible owner	Incident management process owner	Service improvement manager	Service and Service improvement manager
Authorize or rejected process document	Senior responsible owner	Service improvement manager	-	Document librarian

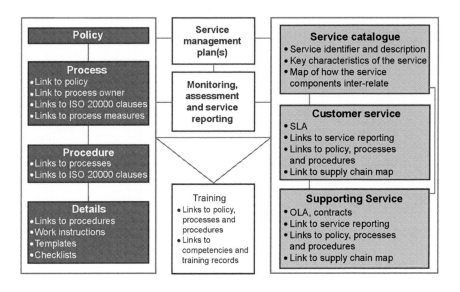

Figure 10 – Document structure for ISO/IEC 20000

Document libraries

Defining the relationships between documents is simplified by:

- grouping related documents into a logical set, e.g. a folder;

- referencing dependent documents in a document;

- defining the relationships in configuration management.

Changes must ripple through all related documents and records. For example, when a change to process is agreed, any affected training material is also changed.

Auditors will expect documents and records to be grouped in an orderly structure, providing evidence of a logical, rather than haphazard, approach to document and record management. Table 8 provides an example systematic approach as a three level hierarchy.

Table 8 – Grouping documents and records

Level 1	Level 2	Documents and records
Management products	By process, e.g. change management	Process management plan Process improvement plan Audit report for the process Post-implementation review report
	By service, e.g. desktop service	Service management plan Audit report Post-implementation review report
Staffing	Staff development	Staff competencies by role Training plan
	Training material by topic, e.g. process	Training presentation Competency questionnaire
Customer service	By customer service, e.g. payroll service	Service requirements specification Service level requirement specification Service level agreement Service report template(s)

Some service providers include a table in the document control procedure that shows where each type of document and record is physically held. Alternatively, or as a supplement, a graphical representation may be used, such as the example in Figure 11. This is a representation of part of the hierarchical relationships between policy, process and process objectives and procedures, with supporting details. In this example, the links joining the boxes represents hyperlinks if the documents are on an intranet, or manual cross-references.

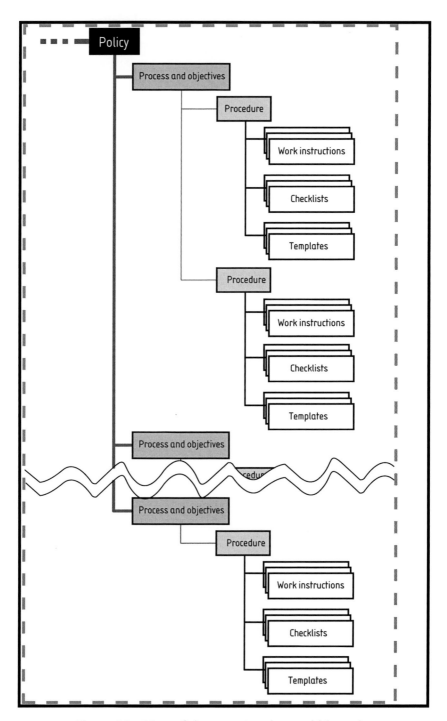

Figure 11 – Map of document and record hierarchy

Communicating changes to documents

One of the most fundamental but regrettably common omissions is the failure to communicate to staff about the policies, processes and procedures, including document management. Staff are left not knowing about new ways of working. A gap opens between how the document describes activities and what is actually done in practice.

Housekeeping and retention

The requirements for access and control are not achievable without best practice document housekeeping and retention periods.

Protection and security

ISO/IEC 20000-2 recommends that documentation should be protected. For example, documents and records protected from a virus or unapproved access. BIP 0036, *Keeping the service going*, describes how documents should be included in service continuity planning.

Disposal methods may need to cater for information being confidential or potentially exposing the service provider, customer or suppliers to security risks. This necessary caution applies to both electronic and hard copy formats.

Legal and regulatory requirements

Although not included in ISO/IEC 20000 requirements, legal and regulatory requirements should also be taken into account.

Most requirements stipulate a number of years that documents and records to be retained to provide evidence of the controls applied to information changes. Where electronic media is used consideration should be given to the rate of media degradation, the availability of devices, obsolescence of storage media and the speed and nature of access required.

The service provider must also be alert to regulations and legislation on personal information, including that about their own staff.

Example metrics and audit evidence

Example metrics and audit evidence are given in Tables 9 and 10.

Table 9 – Example metrics relating to documentation

Metric	Type of Metric	Purpose and objectives
Effective control	Time taken to update and disseminate the change to documents, once the change has been agreed Number of incidents caused by deficient documentation and record keeping	Service providers shall provide documentation and records to ensure effective ... control ... of service management
Document control	Decreased number of non-conformance reports against documentation Number and percentage of documents used in specified period	Procedures and responsibilities shall be established for the creation, review, approval, maintenance, control and disposal of the various types of documents and records

Table 10 – Example audit evidence for requirements

Objective and requirement	Example audit evidence
Objective: To provide a management system, including policies and a framework to enable the effective management and implementation of all IT services.	
Service providers **shall** provide documents and records to ensure effective planning, operation and control of service management	• Documentation includes policies and plans for effective planning • Documentation is used to effectively plan and control service management e.g. SLA and service reports • Actions completed from minutes of meetings
Procedures and responsibilities **shall** be established for the creation, review, approval, maintenance, control and disposal of the various types of documents and records	• Documentation plan and/or configuration management plan that includes documentation • Documentation control procedures • Document index and linked controlled document libraries

CHAPTER 9

Using ISO/IEC 20000 to select a service provider

Unlike the rest of this publication, which is written from the perspective of a service provider interested in achieving compliance with ISO/IEC 20000, this chapter is written from the perspective of the customer, who may choose to use ISO/IEC 20000 as a quality standard for their suppliers. This can be part of the procurement process as a means of selecting the successful provider or as a measure of the service provider once in place. It is commonly both.

Using ISO/IEC 20000 in the procurement process

Outsourcing tenders and contracts have included references to, and requirements based on, ISO/IEC 20000. The simplest requirement is for the prospective service provider to demonstrate compliance with ISO/IEC 20000 for existing services or to commit to achieving the ISO/IEC 20000 standard within a specified period after contract signature.

Where there are several organizations contributing part of the overall service, a relatively common circumstance, the customer may opt to request that a lead supplier demonstrates that their processes conform to ISO/IEC 20000. Under these circumstances the lead supplier is then the service provider aiming to achieve ISO/IEC 20000. This service provider/lead supplier must also demonstrate that they are in turn managing the service from any subcontracted suppliers, so that the overall service meets the contractual requirements of their customer. This is described in more detail in BIP 0033, *Managing end-to-end service*.

Alternatively, the customer may opt for placing a separate obligation on all suppliers so that each in turn is a service provider aiming to achieve ISO/IEC 20000. This is inherently more complex to manage from the customer's perspective and may result in a higher cost for the supplier management process. However, this approach gives greater direct control over the service.

This approach of separate obligations for all suppliers may also put a barrier in the way for suppliers who are so specialized that they cannot achieve compliance with the scoping requirements. Under these circumstances requiring ISO/IEC 20000 of all suppliers may be not be sensible or productive for the customer. Each approach should be considered in the context of the needs and benefits for the customer's organization.

Although ISO/IEC 20000 includes no requirements of customers, when a customer decides to place an obligation on their service providers to achieve ISO/IEC 20000, this should also be done with the full recognition that this impacts the customer's own policies, processes and procedures. For example, among many other examples, the business relationship process requires the service provider to track customer satisfaction, this can only be done if the customer's organization cooperates.

In addition it is advisable to:

- ensure that the service provider's management team are committed to and actively involved in delivering the required quality of service;

- ensure that your own organization is also committed to dealing with the service provider in accordance with the requirements of ISO/IEC 20000, particularly relationship management;

- understand the cultural fit of the prospective supplier with your own organization.

Using ISO/IEC 20000 requirements as a checklist

When defining the requirements of a supplier (both internal and external) the customer will find the specification of good practices in ISO/IEC 20000 useful. At its most basic, ISO/IEC 20000 can be used as a checklist. Specific key requirements of ISO/IEC 20000 can be included in a description of the service required in an invitation to tender document or in the actual contract.

Relying on ISO/IEC 20000 certificates

If you are relying on an existing ISO/IEC 20000 certificate when selecting a supplier, you are advised to check the following.

- Was the audit a full certification audit by an independent professional audit company, as described in Chapter 4, *Compliance and certification audits*?

- If this is the case, the certificate will say so and include the official logo for the certification scheme.

- Is the service provider capable of delivering the required quality of service for all your required services and all your required locations.

- Was the scope of the certification audit so narrow that it may not match the requirements for your organization, e.g. in terms of location and type of service?

The assessment may have been carried out by an organization that is not a professional audit company, or an audit company that has not got the specific experience in service management required. This type of organization will not be registered under a recognized ISO/IEC 20000 certification scheme.

Service providers may also claim compliance with ISO/IEC 20000, but on the basis of self-certification, i.e. they themselves have assessed their service management and believe they meet requirements. This is not a certification audit and this type of audit cannot be guaranteed to be independent or to have been carried out with the rigour required.

CHAPTER **10**

Terminology in ISO/IEC 20000 and certification schemes

Introduction

The following terms and definitions are used in the standards and certification industries. This chapter also includes the 15 terms and definitions included in ISO/IEC 20000-1. All other terms are words used as per the definitions given in commonly available English language dictionaries.

Spelling

Spelling in international standards sometimes triggers comments about what is assumed to be incorrect UK English spelling. For example, organization, not organisation (but analyse, not analyze). It is not, as is sometimes assumed, the adoption of US English, e.g. organization. Spelling in international standards is as found in the Shorter Oxford English Dictionary. This lists both 'organisation' and 'organization' as valid spellings, i.e. the word is acceptable with either 's' or 'z'. The use of organization was historically more common than the use of 'organisation'.

The use of 'z' was adopted many years ago in the US and this usage has not changed over time. In the UK, common spelling has been influenced by French spelling in which 's' is more common than 'z' for many words. This resulted in common use changing over time from 'organization' to 'organisation'.

Although the use of 'z' is unusual in UK English it is correct and it is this form that has been adopted for national and international standards.

Terms, definitions and organizations

accreditation body
assesses organizations that provide certification, testing, inspection and calibration services. Accreditation by an accreditation body demonstrates the competence, impartiality and performance capability of an organization that does audits. This is to ensure there is a consistent approach to **certification** audits by **accredited certification bodies**. Examples of accreditation bodies include RvA (The Netherlands), JAB (Japan) and UKAS (UK). Many **accredited certification bodies** that work outside the UK are registered with UKAS and may be registered with several other national accreditation bodies.

The relationship between the various bodies is as shown below.

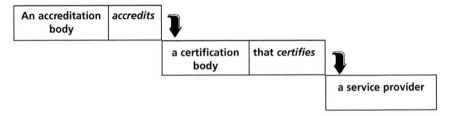

accredited certification body
organization that performs **certification** audits, commonly referred to as 'professional audit companies' and which has been accredited by an accreditation body.

accreditation procedure
by which a body such as the **International Accreditation Forum, Inc. (IAF)** or the **European Cooperation for Accreditation (EA)** gives formal recognition that a body or person is competent to carry out specific tasks and will do so impartially. In this context the task is an ISO/IEC 20000 **certification** audit. The accreditation procedure ensures that the registration that follows when the accreditation procedure is successful is recognized throughout the world.

availability (ISO/IEC 20000-1, 2.1)
ability of a component or service to perform its required function at a stated instant or over a stated period of time.

NOTE Availability is usually expressed as a ratio of the time that the service is actually available for use by the business to the agreed service hours.

baseline (ISO/IEC 20000-1, 2.2)
snapshot of the state of a service or individual **configuration items** at a point in time.

can
verb form that is used only for 'statements of possibility and capability'.

certification
procedure by which a third-party gives written assurance that a product, process or service conforms to specified requirements. ISO/IEC 20000 certification means meeting the specified requirements following an independent audit by an **accredited certification body**, i.e. an audit company/auditors who are formally qualified and registered to carry out ISO/IEC 20000 audits.

certification body
see accredited certification body.

change record (ISO/IEC 20000-1, 2.3)
record containing details of which **configuration items** are affected and how they are affected by an authorized change.

code of practice
a standard that recommends 'good, accepted practice as followed by competent practitioners'. Recommendations in a code of practice use the auxiliary **'should'**. A code of practice will not contain the verb form **'shall'**.

compliance
meeting the requirements in ISO/IEC 20000 (or other national or international standards), as assessed by an internal audit or an organization that is not an **accredited certification body** or qualified to carry out ISO/IEC 20000 certification audits. Compliance includes 'Self-certification audits'.

configuration item (CI) (ISO/IEC 20000-1, 2.4)
component of an infrastructure or an item which is, or will be, under the control of configuration management.

NOTE Configuration items may vary widely in complexity, size and type, ranging from an entire system including all hardware, software and documentation, to a single module or a minor hardware component.

configuration management database (CMDB) (ISO/IEC 20000-1, 2.5)
database containing all the relevant details of each configuration item and details of the important relationships between them.

document (ISO/IEC 20000-1, 2.6)
information and its supporting medium.

NOTE 1 **records** are distinguished from documents by the fact that they function as evidence of activities, rather than evidence of intentions.

NOTE 2 Examples of documents include policy statements, plans, procedures, service level agreements and contracts.

European Cooperation for Accreditation (EA)

exists to ensure that there is a uniform approach to accreditation throughout Europe and that there is universal acceptance of accredited certificates and reports *(see International Accreditation Forum (IAF))*.

incident (ISO/IEC 20000-1, 2.7)

any event which is not part of the standard operation of a service and which causes or may cause an interruption to, or a reduction in, the quality of that service.

NOTE This may include request questions such as "How do I...?" calls.

International Accreditation Forum, Inc. (IAF)

global association of conformity assessment accreditation bodies and other bodies involved in conformity assessment in the field of management systems, products, services and personnel. Members of IAF are **national accreditation bodies,** often abbrieviated to accreditation bodies.

In very simple terms this is an association of organizations whos core business is to check and control the consistency of how audit companies actually do audits. In this context 'audit companies' are **accredited certification bodies**.

In the case of IAF, it's primary function is to develop a single worldwide programme of conformity assessment which reduces risk for business and its customers by assuring them that accredited certificates may be relied upon. There are over 40 **national accreditation bodies** who are members of IAF, including **ANAB** (USA), **CNAB** (China), **DAR** (Germany), **JAB** (Japan) **Accreditation Board for Conformity Assessment** JAS-ANZ: JAS-ANZ (joint Australia and new Zealand), **RvA** (The Netherlands), **SANAS** (South Africa), **SINCERT-FIDEA** (Italy) to **UKAS** (UK).

may

verb form that indicates 'permissibility within the limits of a standard (or a specific course of action' The word 'may' is used several times before the requirements clauses 3 to 10 of ISO/IEC 2000-1, but only once in the requirements, in clause 7.3, Business relationship management. It appears in the sentence 'Other stakeholders in the service may also be invited to the meetings'. This indicates that other stakeholders being invited to meetings will not conflict with the requirements, but that this is not in itself a requirement, i.e. it is not a 'shall'. May is used several times in ISO/IEC 20000-2, and represents a form of advice.

must

auxiliary verb that is not used in standards 'in order to avoid confusion between the requirements of the standard and external statutory obligations'. The word 'must' does not appear in ISO/IEC 20000.

national accreditation body
see accreditation body.

normative
indicating compulsory provisions in a standard (as opposed to informative provisions which are purely there for information).

notes
informative text important to the understanding of a provision in the document. A note will not contain any requirements. In a specification, such as ISO/IEC 20000-1 a note is similar in meaning to the advice and guidance provided by a code of practice such as ISO/IEC 20000-2. Notes in a specification can be ignored by a service provider and inclusion does not in any way change the requirements. In the current edition of ISO/IEC 20000-2 some notes have been introduced to allow unique cross-references where a sub clause would otherwise include more than one alpha list. Conversion of normal text to a note in the code of practice does not change the status of the advice or guidance.

objectives
brief statements used in both parts of ISO/IEC 20000. They are included to assist in the understanding of each process and do not form part of the requirements, even in the specification ISO/IEC 20000-1. Objectives are similar to notes (see above). However, a service provider will normally find the objectives useful input when establishing policies and planning service management.

policy, process and procedure
essential components of the audit evidence that describes the best practices requirements of ISO/IEC 20000, each being linked in a logical hierarchy of policy under-pinned by processes, which are under-pinned by procedures. When a procedure is documented, the term 'written procedure' or 'documented procedure' is frequently used. In ISO/IEC 20000 all policies, processes and procedures referred to are formally documented, so the ISO/IEC 20000 does not qualify policies, processes and procedures as 'written procedures' or 'formal procedures'. The three terms are used as in other management system standards:

- **policy**: the overall intentions and direction of a service provider formally expressed by senior management;

- **process**: an activity using resources to transform inputs to outputs. Often, the output from one process will directly form the input into the next process;

- **procedure:** the specified way to carry out a process.

problem (ISO/IEC 20000-1, 2.8)
unknown underlying cause of one or more incidents.

record (ISO/IEC 20000-1, 2.9)
document stating results achieved or providing evidence of activities performed.

NOTE 1 records are distinguished from **documents** by the fact that they function as evidence of activities, rather than evidence of intentions.

NOTE 2 examples of records include audit reports, requests for change, incident reports, individual training records and invoices sent to customers.

release (ISO/IEC 20000-1, 2.10)
collection of new and/or changed **configuration items** which are tested and introduced into the live environment together.

request for change (ISO/IEC 20000-1, 2.11)
form or screen used to record details of a request for a change to any **configuration item** within a service or infrastructure.

service desk (ISO/IEC 20000-1, 2.12)
customer facing support group who do a high proportion of the total support work.

service level agreement (SLA) (ISO/IEC 20000-1, 2.13)
written agreement between a **service provider** and a customer that documents services and agreed service levels.

service management (ISO/IEC 20000-1, 2.14)
management of services to meet the business requirements.

service provider (ISO/IEC 20000-1, 2.15)
the organization aiming to achieve ISO/IEC 20000.

shall
verb form that identifies **normative provisions** within a **specification**, i.e. the compulsory requirements in ISO/IEC 20000-1. These only occur in clauses 3 to 10. The Introduction, Foreword and clauses 2 and 3 do not form part of the requirements irrespective of how they are worded. 'Shall' is not used in clauses 3 onwards in ISO/IEC 20000-2.

should
verb form that identifies a recommendation, i.e. the guidance provisions in ISO/IEC 20000-2. This is used extensively in ISO/IEC 20000-2. In ISO/IEC 20000-1 the word 'should' occurs only in the NOTEs, as these represent explanations similar to the advice in ISO/IEC 20000-2.

specification

a standard that sets out 'detailed requirements, using the prescriptive **'shall'**, to be satisfied by a product, material process or system'.

In ISO/IEC 20000 the verbs **shall** (and **should**) refer to aspects of the management processes, **also including policy, procedures**, plans and **objectives.**

ISO/IEC 20000 requirements in summary

It is important to refer to ISO/IEC 20000-1 and ISO/IEC 20000-2 and not rely only on the abstract given here, which covers those parts of the ISO/IEC 20000 that are particularly pertinent to management responsibilities and management decision making.

Other publications in the 'Achieving ISO/IEC 20000' series feature similar tables covering other requirements in the same way.

Each requirement (signified by the use of the verb **'shall'**) is supplemented by informative commentary based on the details in ISO/IEC 20000-2 and related publications (see the *Bibliography* in Appendix B).

Table A.1 — ISO/IEC 20000 requirements with informative commentary/guidance

ISO/IEC 20000-1 requirements	ISO/IEC 20000-2 recommendations (*italics*) and additional commentary (**bold**)
Clause 3 Requirements for a management system *Objective: To provide a management system, including policies and a framework to enable the effective management and implementation of all IT services.* **Clause 3.1 Management responsibility** Through leadership and actions, top/executive management **shall** provide evidence of its commitment to developing, implementing and improving its service management capability within the context of the organization's business and customers' requirements. Management **shall**: • establish the service management policy, objectives and plans; • communicate the importance of meeting the service management objectives and the need for continual improvement; • ensure that customer requirements are determined and are met with the aim of improving customer satisfaction; • appoint a member of management responsible for the coordination and management of all services;	*The role of management in ensuring best practice processes are adopted and sustained is fundamental for any service provider if they are to meet the requirements of ISO/IEC 20000-1.* **When service management processes are not working effectively, the root cause of failure may be traced back to a lack of commitment from senior management. That lack of commitment may be caused by an inadequate cost-benefit case being presented, typically one without tangible benefits or based on increased costs in the short term, with no evidence that long-term costs will then be less.** **This requirement emphasizes the importance of management commitment to ISO/IEC 20000 and best practice service management. If evidence of this commitment is not found by the auditor during an assessment the service provider will be judged not to have met the requirements of ISO/IEC 20000, however enthusiastic and committed more junior members of staff are to service management best practices and individual processes.** *To ensure commitment, an owner at senior level* **should** *be identified as being responsible for senior management plans. This senior responsible owner* **should** *be accountable for the overall delivery of the service management plan.*

ISO/IEC 20000-1 requirements

- determine and provide resources to plan, implement, monitor, review and improve service delivery and management e.g. recruit appropriate staff, manage staff turnover;

- manage risks to the service management organization and services; and

- conduct reviews of service management, at planned intervals, to ensure continuing suitability, adequacy and effectiveness.

ISO/IEC 20000-2 recommendations (*italics*) and additional commentary (**bold**)

The senior manager selected for this should also have the time and commitment to service management improvements. A distant figurehead will not be effective, however senior. Some organizations find it helpful to ask for a sponsor in the customer's management team, but this type of sponsorship is not actually specified in ISO/IEC 20000.

The senior responsible owner's role should encompass resourcing for any continual or project based service improvement activities.

It will be an advantage if the manager has control over any necessary budgets or is experienced in making and carrying through funding requests based on cost-benefit analyses.

The senior managers should be supported by a decision making group with sufficient authority to define policy and enforce its decisions.

This will help cascade best practices down through the service provider's organization.

The establishment of a policy on service management is essential for achieving ISO/IEC 20000, and the service provider should be able to show the relationship between policies, processes and procedures as part of a logical structure.

ISO/IEC 20000-2 recommends that service providers should adopt common terminology and a more consistent approach to service management.

This is because failure to understand the terminology can be a barrier to establishing effective and consistent processes. Understanding the terminology is a tangible and significant benefit that can be gained from a ISO/IEC 20000 project.

ISO/IEC 20000-1 requirements	ISO/IEC 20000-2 recommendations (*italics*) and additional commentary (**bold**)

Clause 3.2 Documentation requirements

Documentation requirements

Service providers **shall** provide documents and records to ensure effective planning, operation and control of service management.

The senior responsible owner **should** *ensure that evidence is available for an audit of service management policies, plans and procedures, and any activities related to these.*

This **shall** include:

Much of the evidence of service management planning and operations **should** *exist in the form of documents, which may be any type, form or medium suitable for their purpose.*

- documented service management policies and plans;

The following documents are normally considered suitable as evidence of service management planning:

- documented service level agreements;

a) *policies and plans;*

- documented processes and procedures required by this standard; and

b) *service documentation;*

c) *procedures;*

- records required by this standard.

d) *processes;*

Procedures and responsibilities **shall** be established for the creation, review, approval, maintenance, disposal and control of the various types of documents and records.

e) *process control records.*

Note: the documentation can be in any form or type of medium.

The preparation of documentary evidence for an audit should not be treated as an activity carried out just for an audit. Documents and other records need to be those that are used in the normal course of service management.

It is important to avoid document production as an activity in its own right. Documents, where possible, should be short, to the point, mainly pictures, tables or checklists with the minimum of words.

There **should** *be a process for the creation and management of documents to help ensure that the characteristics described are met.*

ISO/IEC 20000-1 requirements	ISO/IEC 20000-2 recommendations (*italics*) and additional commentary (**bold**)
	Documentation should be protected from damage, e.g. due to poor environmental conditions and computer failures.
	Document and version control is essential and it is normally best to keep documents in a document library with simple rules determining the scope, content and purpose of each document.
	Documentation for ISO/IEC 20000 should be integrated with existing documentation for other management systems that the organization may have adopted, such as ISO 9000 and ISO/IEC 17799 or the ISO/IEC 27000 series. For example, there should *not* be one set of documents for ISO 9000 and one set for ISO/IEC 20000.

Clause 3.3 Competence, awareness and training

All service management roles and responsibilities **shall** be defined and maintained together with the competencies required to execute them effectively.	**General** *Personnel performing work within service management should be competent on the basis of appropriate education, training, skills, and experience.* *The service provider should:* a) *determine the necessary competence for each role in service management;* b) *ensure that personnel are aware of the relevance and importance of their activities within the wider business context and how they contribute to the achievement of quality objectives;* c) *maintain appropriate records of education, training, skills and experience;* d) *provide training or take other action to satisfy these needs;* e) *evaluate the effectiveness of the actions taken.*

ISO/IEC 20000-1 requirements

ISO/IEC 20000-2 recommendations (*italics*) and additional commentary (**bold**)

Professional development

*The service provider **should** develop and enhance the professional competence of their workforce. Among the measures taken to achieve this, the service provider **should** address the following:*

a) *__recruitment__: with the objective of checking the validity of job applicants' details (including their professional qualifications) and identifying applicants' strengths, weaknesses and potential capabilities, against a job description/profile, service management targets and overall service quality objectives;*

b) *__planning__: with the objective of staffing of new or expanded services (also contracting services), using new technology, assigning service management staff to development project teams, succession planning and filling other gaps due to anticipated staff turnover;*

c) *__training and development__: with the objective of identifying training and development requirements as a training and development plan and providing for timely and effective delivery.*

*Staff **should** be trained in the relevant aspects of service management (e.g. via training courses, self study, mentoring and on the job training) and their team-working and leadership skills **should** be developed. A chronological training record **should** be maintained for each individual, together with descriptions of the training provided.*

Approaches to be considered

*In order to achieve teams of staff with appropriate levels of competence the service provider **should** decide on the optimum mix of short term and permanent recruits. The service provider **should** also decide on the optimum mix of new staff with the skills required and re-training of existing staff.*

ISO/IEC 20000-1 requirements

ISO/IEC 20000-2 recommendations (*italics*) and additional commentary (bold)

NOTE   The optimum balance of short term and permanent recruits is particularly important when the service provider is planning how to provide a service during and after major changes to the number and skills of the support staff.

*Factors that **should** be considered when establishing the most suitable combination of approaches include:*

a) *short or long term nature of new or changed competencies;*

b) *rate of change in the skills and competencies;*

c) *expected peaks and troughs in the workload and skills mix required, based on service management and service improvement planning;*

d) *availability of suitably competent staff;*

e) *staff turnover rates;*

f) *training plans.*

Although there is no requirement to use any particular technique for mapping roles and responsibilities specified in ISO/IEC 20000, responsibility matrices are ideal for this purpose. They clearly illustrate the interfaces between roles and clarify the responsibilities of each role to avoid gaps and set expectations, thus reducing the risk to the service. Production of matrices forces clarity on who does what and when. Examples of responsibility matrices are given in BIP 0031, *Why people matter*.

ISO/IEC 20000-1 requirements

Staff competencies and training needs **shall** be reviewed and managed to enable staff to perform their role effectively.

Top management **shall** ensure that its employees are aware of the relevance and importance of their activities and how they contribute to the achievement of the service management objectives.

ISO/IEC 20000-2 recommendations (*italics*) and additional commentary (**bold**)

For all staff, the service provider should review each individual's performance at least annually and take appropriate action.

Service management objectives can be incorporated into staff appraisals and job descriptions. This reduces confusion and is essential for effective service management, particularly for the continuous improvement required even after ISO/IEC 20000 has been achieved.

Well-defined roles, together with their functions and responsibilities, are essential to ensure all staff understand the role they play. This may take the form of job descriptions or procedure documents and can be supported by roles and responsibility matrices, as described in BIP 0031, *Why people matter*.

ISO/IEC 20000-1 requirements	ISO/IEC 20000-2 recommendations (*italics*) and additional commentary (**bold**)

Clause 4 Planning and implementing service management

Clause 4.1 Plan service management (Plan)

Objective: To plan the implementation and delivery of service management.

Plan-Do-Check-Act methodology for service management processes

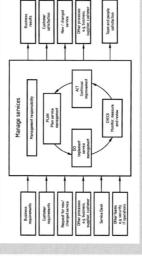

The model shown in Figure 2 illustrates the process and process linkages presented in clauses 4 to 10.

Service management **shall** be planned.

For an organization to function effectively it has to identify and manage numerous linked activities. Co-ordinated integration and implementation of the service management processes provides the ongoing control, greater efficiency and opportunities for continuous improvement.

ISO/IEC 20000-1 requirements	ISO/IEC 20000-2 recommendations (*italics*) and additional commentary (**bold**)
	Planning is essential for this to happen.
	NOTE This requirement for service management planning is part of PDCA. As a requirement it is separate from the change management process which plans operational changes.
	Scope of service management
	The scope of service management **should** *be defined in the service management plan. For example, it may be defined by:*
	• *organization;*
	• *location;*
	• *service.*
	Management **should** *define the scope as part of their management responsibilities (and as part of the service management plan). The scope* **should** *then be checked for suitability under ISO/IEC 20000-1.*
	NOTE Planning for operational changes is described in 9.2.
	Planning approaches
	Multiple service management plans may be used in place of one large plan or programme. Where this is the case the underlying service management processes **should** *be consistent with each other. It* **should** *also be possible to demonstrate how each planning requirement is managed by linking it to the corresponding roles, responsibilities and procedures.*
	Service management planning **should** *form part of the process for translating customers' requirements and senior management intentions into services, and for providing a route map for directing progress.*

ISO/IEC 20000-1 requirements

The plans **shall** at a minimum define:

a) the scope of the service provider's service management;

b) the objectives and requirements that are to be achieved by service management;

c) the processes that are to be executed;

d) the framework of management roles and responsibilities, including the senior responsible owner, process owner and management of suppliers;

e) the interfaces between service management processes and the manner in which the activities are to be coordinated;

f) the approach to be taken in identifying, assessing and managing issues and risks to the achievement of the defined objectives;

g) the approach for interfacing to projects that are creating or modifying services;

h) the resources, facilities and budget necessary to achieve the defined objectives;

ISO/IEC 20000-2 recommendations (*italics*) and additional commentary (**bold**)

*A service management plan **should** encompass:*

a) *implementation of service management (or part of service management);*

b) *delivery of service management processes;*

c) *changes to service management processes;*

d) *improvements to service management processes;*

e) *new services (to the extent that they affect processes within the agreed scope of service management).*

Events to be considered

The service management plan should cater for service management process and service changes triggered by events such as:

a) *service improvement*

b) *service changes*

c) *infrastructure standardization;*

d) *changes to legislation;*

e) *regulatory changes, e.g. local tax rate changes;*

f) *deregulation or regulation of industries;*

g) *mergers and acquisitions.*

ISO/IEC 20000-2 recommendations (*italics*) and additional commentary (**bold**)

Scope and contents of the plan

*A service management plan **should** define:*

a) *the scope of service provider's service management;*

b) *the objectives and requirements that are to be achieved;*

c) *the resources, facilities and budgets necessary to achieve the defined objectives;*

d) *the framework of management roles and responsibilities, including the senior responsible owner, process owners and management of suppliers;*

e) *the interfaces between service management processes and the manner in which the activities and/or processes are to be coordinated;*

f) *the approach to be taken in identifying, assessing and managing issues and risks to the achievement of the defined objectives;*

g) *a resource schedule expressed in terms of the dates on which funds, skills, and resources **should** be available;*

h) *the approach to changing the plan and the service defined by the plan;*

i) *how the service provider will demonstrate continuing quality control (e.g. interim audits).*

This is a standard requirement of any project plan and is especially important to service management implementation, change and improvements, in view of the number of people involved or affected in service management plans. This is not, however, a requirement for a very detailed plan with voluminous background documents. A plan which is simple, well executed and well understood is more likely to be effective.

ISO/IEC 20000-1 requirements

i) tools as appropriate to support the processes; and

j) how the quality of the service will be managed, audited and improved.

There **shall** be clear management direction and documented responsibilities for reviewing, authorizing, communicating, implementing and maintaining the plans.

112

ISO/IEC 20000-1 requirements

Any process specific plans produced **shall** be compatible with this service management plan.

ISO/IEC 20000-2 recommendations (*italics*) and additional commentary (**bold**)

Where separate plans are used, these must be linked and the service management processes should be consistent with each other.

It is particularly important to track the interfaces and data flows between processes if multiple plans are used.

It should also be possible to demonstrate how each planning requirement is managed by linking it to the corresponding roles, responsibilities and procedures.

Clause 4.2 Implement service management and provide the services (Do)

Objective: To implement the service management objectives and plan.

The service provider **shall** implement the service management plan to manage and deliver the services, including:

a) allocation of funds and budgets;

b) allocation of roles and responsibilities;

c) documenting and maintaining the policies, plans, procedures and definitions for each process or set of processes;

d) identification and management of risks to the service;

e) managing teams, e.g. recruiting and developing appropriate staff and managing staff continuity;

Attainment of best practice service management processes capable of meeting the requirements of ISO/IEC 20000 will not be achieved if the original services do not meet the requirements outlined for the implementation in ISO/IEC 20000-1.

Once implemented the service and service management processes **should** *be maintained with the same level of rigour used in the original service management plan.*

Reviews **should** *take place in accordance with clause 4.3 (below).*

NOTE The person that is appropriate for the planning and initial implementation may not be suitable for the ongoing operation.

This is a feature of other service management roles. For some roles, a person who has a preference for a rapid cycle of events is most appropriate for working in one of the more reactive roles, conversely, some people are happier planning and prefer the

ISO/IEC 20000-1 requirements	ISO/IEC 20000-2 recommendations (*italics*) and additional commentary (**bold**)
f) managing facilities and budget; g) managing the teams including service desk and operations; h) reporting progress against the plans; and coordination of service management processes.	**longer terms roles, such as continuity management. For all aspects of service management, roles and personalities need to match.** **These ISO/IEC 20000 requirements will only be successful if the planning stage, described previously, is carried out thoroughly.**

Clause 4.3 Monitoring, measuring and reviewing (Check)

Objective: To monitor, measure and review that the service management objectives and plan are being achieved.

The service provider **shall** apply suitable methods for monitoring and, where applicable, measurement of the service management processes. These methods **shall** demonstrate the ability of the processes to achieve planned results.	*The service provide **should** plan and implement the monitoring, measurement and analysis of the service, the service management processes and associated systems.* *The results of the analysis **should** provide input to the service improvement programme.* *Items that **should** be monitored, measured and reviewed include:* *a) achievement against defined service targets;* *b) customer satisfaction;* *c) resource utilisation;* *d) trends;* *e) major nonconformities;* *The results of the analysis **should** provide input to a plan for improving the service* **The subject of measures is covered in detail in BIP 0032, *Making metrics work*.**

ISO/IEC 20000-1 requirements	ISO/IEC 20000-2 recommendations (*italics*) and additional commentary (**bold**)
Management **shall** conduct reviews at planned intervals to determine whether the service management requirements: a) conform with the service management plan and to the requirements of this standard; b) are effectively implemented and maintained.	*As well as service management activities on measurement and analysis senior management may need to make use of internal audits and other checks.* **This has been covered in Chapters 4 and 7.** **The subject of service reviews, involving customers, has been described in BIP 0033, Managing end-to-end service.**
An audit programme **shall** be planned, taking into consideration the status and importance of the processes and areas to be audited, as well as the results of previous audits.	*When deciding the frequency of internal audits and checks, the degree of risk involved in a process, its frequency of operation and its past history of problems are among the factors that should be taken into account.*
The audit criteria, scope, frequency and methods **shall** be defined in a procedure.	
The selection of auditors and conduct of audits **shall** ensure objectivity and impartiality of the audit process.	*Internal audits and checks should be planned, carried out competently and recorded.*
Auditors **shall** not audit their own work.	**Only informal internal assessments should be carried out by the person responsible for the process being audited. However, each manager may be asked to audit another manager's processes. This can cause conflict unless there is a good team spirit but it does help develop a common understanding of what each team deals with.**

ISO/IEC 20000-1 requirements	ISO/IEC 20000-2 recommendations (*italics*) and additional commentary (**bold**)
The objective of service management reviews, assessments and audits **shall** be recorded together with the findings of such audits and reviews and any remedial actions identified.	**This does not need to be a voluminous report, a template of key features and a method of summarizing the results is helpful if a group of people are involved. This has similarities to the approach that is adopted to ensure certification audits are carried out in a consistent and fair manner, but it can be adapted to the needs of a specific organization that may not be aiming for certification but wish to use parts of ISO/IEC 20000 to establish service improvement goals.** **BIP 0033, *Managing end-to-end service* covers the subject of service reviews.**
Any significant areas of non-compliance or concern **shall** be communicated to relevant parties.	**Where an audit is a formal certification audit, communication of non-compliance will be part of the process. However, if a less formal audit or a processes assessment is being carried out based on ISO/IEC 20000, there should be a process for gauging feedback on any concern, service improvement suggestion or complaint. This can be a simple mechanism ensuring that the process owner is informed of any concerns (via normal escalation mapping). Change management will also need to be informed as these concerns will be input into the continuous service improvement process.**

Clause 4.4 Continual improvement (Act)

Objective: To improve the effectiveness and efficiency of service delivery and management.

Policy	Policy
There **shall** be a published policy on service improvement.	*Service providers **should** recognize that there is always the potential to improve delivery of services and make them more effective and efficient.* *There **should** be a published policy on service quality and improvement.*

ISO/IEC 20000-1 requirements	ISO/IEC 20000-2 recommendations (*italics*) and additional commentary (**bold**)
	All of those involved **should** *be aware of the service quality policy and their personal contribution to meeting the objectives laid out within this policy.*
	In particular, all of the service provider's staff who are involved **should** *have a detailed understanding of the implications of the published policy on the service management processes.*
	There **should** *be effective liaison between the service provider's own management structure, customers and the service provider's suppliers on matters that affect service quality and customer requirements.*
	The agreement on any policy is important as it sets out the direction for all underlying and linked processes and procedures. A policy is the representation of a business need and can be linked to an organization's strategy.
Any non-compliance with the standard or the service management plans **shall** be remedied.	**Planning for service improvements** *Service providers* **should** *adopt a methodical and coordinated approach to service improvement to meet the requirements of the policy, from their own perspective and from their customers' perspective.* **Good practices in project management as well as service management are required.**
Roles and responsibilities for service improvement activities shall be clearly defined.	**See the details of responsibility matrices illustrated in BIP 0031, *Why people matter.***

117

ISO/IEC 20000-1 requirements	ISO/IEC 20000-2 recommendations (*italics*) and additional commentary (**bold**)
Management of improvements All suggested service improvements **shall** be assessed, recorded, prioritized and authorized. A plan **shall** be used to control the activity.	*Service improvement requirements can be generated from all processes.* **In addition to the service management processes, there can be many different sources for service improvement suggestions, ranging from a specific process (e.g. problem management), post implementation reviews, staff suggestion schemes or customer complaints. All are perfectly valid routes for input to service improvements.** *Service providers should encourage their staff and customers to suggest ways of improving services.* **The key requirement is not what source they come from but that they are handled in a properly controlled manner. This also applies to any (potential) changes.** **The change management process describes a method of providing rigour throughout the various improvements. Some of these improvements may conflict, in which case they can be usefully batched so that the overhead of managing the implementation of the improvements is controlled as well as possible.**
The service provider **shall** have a process in place to identify, measure, report and manage improvement activities on an ongoing basis. This **shall** include: a) improvements to an individual process that can be implemented by the process owner with the usual	**Service improvement, like any change to the service, needs to be assessed for the value it will deliver compared to the cost and (usually) the short-term risk of making the change. To carry this out it is necessary to identify and measure, if available, performance indicators of the service before and after the change. When performance indicators are available it is possible to learn from experience and ensure that future changes originate from a firmly planned and business-like basis.**

ISO/IEC 20000-1 requirements

staff resources, e.g. performing individual corrective and preventive actions; and

b) improvements across the organization or across more than one process.

Activities

The service provider **shall** perform activities to:

a) collect and analyse data to baseline and benchmark service provider's capability to manage and deliver service and service management processes;

b) identify, plan and implement improvements;

c) consult with all parties involved;

d) set targets for improvements in quality, costs and resource utilization;

e) consider relevant inputs about improvements from all the service management processes;

f) measure, report and communicate the service improvements;

g) revise the service management policies, processes, procedures and plans where necessary; and

h) ensure that all approved actions are delivered and that they achieve their intended objectives.

ISO/IEC 20000-2 recommendations (*italics*) and additional commentary (**bold**)

*Service improvement targets **should** be measurable, linked to business objectives and documented in a plan.*

*Service improvements **should** be actively managed and progress **should** be monitored against formally agreed objectives.*

*Before implementing a plan for improving the service, service quality and levels **should** be recorded as a baseline against which the actual improvements can be compared.*

*The actual improvement **should** be compared to the predicted improvement to assess the effectiveness of the change.*

This is covered in more detail in BIP 0032, *Making metrics work*.

ISO/IEC 20000-1 requirements

Major service improvements **shall** be managed as a project or several projects.

ISO/IEC 20000-2 recommendations (*italics*) and additional commentary (bold)

The service provider needs to be able to manage changes to the service, including major service improvements, so that the expected benefits are actually delivered and the service is not at risk. A project or series of projects will be required for this and so it is important that any series of projects (which may be far more effective than a single monolithic change) are coordinated. All of the normal disciplines of good project management are required for this kind of change and will be checked by a professional ISO/IEC 20000 auditor.

Clause 5 Planning and implementing new or changed services

Objective: To ensure that new services and changes to services will be deliverable and manageable at the agreed cost and service quality.

Proposals for new or changed services **shall** consider the cost, organizational, technical and commercial impact that could result from service delivery and management.

Topics for consideration

*Planning for new or changed services **should** include the review of:*

a) *budgets;*

b) *staff resources;*

c) *existing service levels;*

d) *SLAs and other targets or service commitments;*

e) *existing service management processes, procedures and documentation;*

f) *the scope of service management, including the implementation of service management processes previously excluded from the scope.*

ISO/IEC 20000-1 requirements	ISO/IEC 20000-2 recommendations (*italics*) and additional commentary (**bold**)
The implementation of new or changed services, including closure of a service, **shall** be planned and approved through formal change management.	**Change records** *All service changes should be reflected in change management records.*
The planning and implementation **shall** include adequate funding and resources to make the changes needed for service delivery and management.	*This includes plans for:* *a) staff recruitment/retraining;* *b) relocation;* *c) user training;* *d) communications about the changes;* *e) the technology needed to support the changes;* *f) formal closure of services.*
The plans **shall** include: a) the roles and responsibilities for implementing, operating and maintaining the new or changed service including activities to be performed by customers and suppliers; b) changes to the existing service management framework and services; c) communication to the relevant parties; d) new or changed contracts and agreements to align with the changes in business need;	**As previously mentioned, responsibility matrices represent a compact form of identifying who should do what and when. They are an ideal tool for this purpose. Developing a responsibility matrix frequently highlights areas of ambiguity that represent a risk. These ambiguities could be seen by an auditor as a negative aspect of the service management processes being assessed.** **Illustrations of responsibility matrices are given in BIP 0031, *Why people matter*.**

ISO/IEC 20000-1 requirements	ISO/IEC 20000-2 recommendations (*italics*) and additional commentary (**bold**)
e) manpower and recruitment requirements;	
f) skills and training requirements, e.g. users, technical support;	
g) processes, measures, methods and tools to be used in connection with the new or changed service, e.g. capacity management, financial management;	
h) budgets and timescales;	
i) service acceptance criteria; and	
j) the expected outcomes from operating the new service expressed in measurable terms.	
New or changed services **shall** be accepted by the service provider before being implemented into the live environment.	
The service provider **shall** report on the outcomes achieved by the new or changed service against those planned following its implementation.	

ISO/IEC 20000-1 requirements	ISO/IEC 20000-2 recommendations (*italics*) and additional commentary (**bold**)
A post implementation review comparing actual outcomes against those planned, **shall** be performed through the change management process.	**This is standard practice for a project. It is important for improvements in service management that the views of the customer (e.g. via a customer satisfaction survey and service reviews) are taken into account when judging the success (or otherwise) of the improvements.** **Baselining or benchmarking before and after major changes, such as new processes being implemented or changed, is also recommended as part of achieving ISO/IEC 20000. Service management itself provides the mechanisms for this (change management being a process in the scope of ISO/IEC 20000).**

Appendix B

Bibliography and further information

Standards

BS 0-3, *A standard for standards — Part 3: Specification for structure, drafting and presentation*

ISO/IEC Directives Part 2, *Rules for the structure and drafting of International Standards*

ISO 9000, *Quality management systems — Fundamentals and vocabulary*

ISO 9001, *Quality management systems — Requirements*

ISO/IEC 17799, *Information technology — Security techniques — Code of practice for information security management*

ISO/IEC 20000-1, *Information technology — Service management — Part 1: Specification*

ISO/IEC 20000-2, *Information technology — Service management — Part 2: Code of practice*

ISO/IEC 27001, *Information technology — Security techniques — Information security management systems — Requirements*

BSI books

BIP 0005, *A manager's guide to service management*

BIP 0015, *IT service management — Self-assessment workbook*

BIP 0008, *Code of practice for legal admissibility and evidential weight of information stored electronically*

PAS 56, *Guide to business continuity management*

Security information

BIP 0070, *Information security compilation on CD-ROM*

BIP 0071, *Guidelines on requirements and preparation for certification based on ISO/IEC 27001*

BIP 0072, *Are you ready for an ISMS audit based on ISO/IEC 27001?*

BIP 0073, *Guide to the implementation and auditing of ISMS controls based on ISO/IEC 27001*

BIP 0074, *Measuring the effectiveness of your ISMS implementations based on ISO/IEC 27001*

Other resources

British Computer Society: www.bcs.org.uk

British Computer Society Configuration Management Specialist Group: www.bcs-cmsg.org.uk

The IT Service Management Forum (itSMF): www.itsmf.com

EXIN: www.exin.nl

Information Systems Examinations Board (ISEB): www.bcs.org.uk/iseb

The Office of Government Commerce: www.ogc.gov.uk

IT Infrastructure Library (ITIL): www.itil.co.uk

BOOKS IN THE
'ACHIEVING ISO/IEC 20000' SERIES

There are ten books in the 'Achieving ISO/IEC 20000' series. Each book in the series includes an abstract of ISO/IEC 20000 that is most relevant to the topic of the book, as well as useful contacts and sources of supporting information. These books can be purchased through the BSI website at http://eshop.bsi-global.com.

BIP 0030, *Management decisions and documentation*

This book covers: the background to ISO/IEC 20000; a comparison to other standards and best practice material; compliance and certification audits; the scope of service management; building the business case for achieving ISO/IEC 20000; preparation for an audit and using ISO/IEC 20000 to select your supplier. Important terms that are used in management system standards, where the exact meaning of terms is important to the correct interpretation of the standard, are also explained, including the differences between the terms '**shall**', '**should**' and notes. This book also covers the requirements and recommendations for documents and records, which is a management responsibility requirement in clause 3.2 of ISO/IEC 20000-1.

BIP 0031, *Why people matter*

This book covers the roles and responsibilities of management and process owners, and explains the importance of management commitment to best practice service management, mapping onto the requirements and recommendations of clause 3.1 of ISO/IEC 20000, *Management responsibility*. The book also covers the importance of motivation, training and career development as well as tips and techniques, mapping onto the requirements of clause 3.3 of ISO/IEC 20000-1, *Competence, awareness and training*.

BIP 0032, *Making metrics work*

This book gives a practical view of why metrics and service reports are so important to the delivery of an effective service and to service improvements. It describes the types, the design, target audiences and documentation of metrics used in the service reporting process, covered by the requirements of clauses 4 and 6.2 of ISO/IEC 20000-1, *Plan-Do-Check-Act (PDCA) cycle* and *Service reporting*. Useful tips, techniques and example metrics are included.

BIP 0033, *Managing end-to-end service*

This book describes the supply chains that are commonly managed by service level management, business relationship management and supplier management, which are the requirements in clauses 6.1 and 7 of ISO/IEC 20000-1. It describes the interfaces between suppliers, the service provider and one or many customers. This book also includes useful tips for aspects of end-to-end service, such as the role of service level agreements (SLAs), service reviews, customer satisfaction and complaints procedures.

BIP 0034, *Finance for service managers*

This book covers *Budgeting and accounting for IT services* based on clause 6.4 of ISO/IEC 20000. It introduces financial terms that may be unfamiliar to service management specialists, which will help with understanding the requirements and recommendations. It also covers the relationship between budgeting, accounting and charging, and outlines the importance of service management processes in regulatory compliance.

BIP 0035, *Enabling change*

This book covers the configuration, change management and release management processes which are contained in clauses 9 and 10 of ISO/IEC 20000. It compares the three processes and describes how they interface with each other, and gives advice on the requirements and recommendations of ISO/IEC 20000, example metrics and audit evidence. This book also includes practical advice on meeting the ISO/IEC 20000 requirements on the roles and responsibilities of those involved.

BIP 0036, *Keeping the service going*

This book covers the service continuity and availability management, incident management and problem management processes, which are contained in clauses 6.3 and 8 of ISO/IEC 20000. It explains the role of these processes in keeping the customer's service going, ranging from continuity planning through to the fast-fixing of incidents. It compares the processes and describes how they interface with each other. It includes example metrics and audit evidence, with practical tips and techniques that will help a service provider achieve the requirements.

BIP 0037, *Capacity management*

This book covers the requirements for the capacity management process in clause 6.5 of ISO/IEC 20000. It describes the capacity management process and its role as a link between business plans, workloads, capacity and performance). It also covers the planning required to ensure a service provider is able to deliver a service that allows the customer's business to operate effectively. The book describes capacity management for all types of resources within the scope of service management.

BIP 0038, *Integrated service management*

The opening paragraph of ISO/IEC 20000-1 states that '*This standard promotes the adoption of an integrated process approach to effectively deliver managed services to meet the business and customer requirements*'. This book reflects the importance placed by ISO/IEC 20000 on understanding the interfaces between processes, and how the interfaces are managed so that service management processes are fully integrated. It also reflects the top-down management system approach that is fundamental to ISO/IEC 20000. This book describes how understanding and meeting the requirements of ISO/IEC 20000 gives better control, greater efficiency and opportunities for improvements.

BIP 0039, *The differences between BS 15000 and ISO/IEC 20000*

This book will be of particular interest to those who have used BS 15000 for service improvements, audits or training and need to update their material to reflect the ISO/IEC 20000 standard. ISO/IEC 20000 was based on BS 15000, and this book provides a detailed comparison of ISO/IEC 20000 and BS 15000, for both Parts 1 and 2. It shows the differences in structure, clause numbering and references. The core of this book is a series of tables detailing the changes to the requirements and recommendations clause-by-clause, as well as any re-wording that has been provided to give clarification for an international audience. It includes an explanation of why the changes were made and the implications of each of the changes. This book is based on the material produced by the Project Editor during the drafting of both Parts 1 and 2 of ISO/IEC 20000.